fresh*quilting

FEARLESS COLOR, DESIGN & INSPIRATION

MALKA DUBRAWSKY

INTERWEAVE
interweave.com

acknowledgments

→ No project this size is the work of one individual. I may have sewn all the stitches in these projects, but along the way many people have guided and inspired me, and it's my privilege to say thank you.

This book wouldn't be what it is without the patience, enthusiasm, and knowledge of my editor, Elaine Lipson. I also want to express my deepest respect and appreciation to Tricia Waddell for all her encouragement and for always making me feel like my work was special. Thank you to Pokey Bolton and Helen Gregory for their support and a host of opportunities and to Deanna Tollerton for introducing me to the world of long-arm machine quilting, truly a life-changing experience.

For today's crafter, inspiration is often only a mouse click away, and the folks that I've gotten to know via the Internet have wowed me with their artistry and warmed me with their friendship and openness. To Jennifer, Chawne, Erin, Blair, Kathy M., Kathy Y., Amanda, Linda, and Jude, thanks so much.

To my family, Robert, Sarah, Rachel, and Abi, I couldn't create without your love and support. Abi, you especially are my devoted fan and critical eye. I so appreciate your patience as I excitedly make my way through explaining design ideas, never actually completing a sentence, yet you always understand the concept.

A heartfelt thank you to all those who helped make this book a reality via art direction, photography, technical editing, and copyediting. And to all of you who read my words here or on my blog and take the time to let me know what you're thinking and feeling, I thank you for continuing the conversation. — *Malka*

EDITOR Elaine Lipson ✳ **TECHNICAL EDITOR** Rebecca Kemp Brent ✳ **ART DIRECTOR** Liz Quan
COVER + INTERIOR DESIGN Pamela Norman ✳ **PHOTOGRAPHER** Joe Hancock
PHOTO STYLIST Linda Takaha ✳ **HAIR + MAKEUP** Kathy MacKay ✳ **PRODUCTION** Katherine Jackson

Interweave Press LLC, 201 East Fourth Street,
Loveland, CO 80537, interweave.com

Printed in China by Asia Pacific Offset Ltd.

Library of Congress Cataloging-in-Publication Data

Dubrawsky, Malka. Fresh quilting : fearless color, design, and inspiration / Malka Dubrawsky. p. cm. Includes bibliographical references and index.

ISBN 978-1-59668-235-1 (pbk.)

1. Patchwork--Patterns. 2. Quilting--Patterns. I. Title.

TT835.D83 2010 746.46--dc22

2010025314

10 9 8 7 6 5 4 3 2 1

contents

getting fresh *

MY QUILTING STORY

WHEN I was in the third grade, I went with my mother to trade in her saved-up Green Stamps for a sewing machine. I remember how magical the machine seemed to me and being amazed by the quickly formed, perfectly even stitches that emerged as my mother sewed with me sitting beside her.

Those experiences drew me to sewing, even though I didn't really know how. I wasn't even sure that craft was the artistic venue for me. I made brief forays into the sewing world, even handstitching a simple top, but I was convinced early on that though I wanted to pursue art, sewing wasn't really a part of that. Yet even while pursuing a college degree in printmaking, sewing loomed in the back of my mind. I often included elements of sewing patterns in my prints and glued together bits of paper like patchwork quilts.

I finally bought my own sewing machine in my desire to translate those paper quilts into fabric. I envisioned these translations as outgrowths of my prints and drawings and didn't connect them to the world of functional quilts. Then, on a whim, I made a quilt for my bed, and everything changed. Sleeping under that quilt brought back the magical feeling I'd associated with my mother and her machine, but I realized it hadn't been about the machine. Rather, the magic was in the act of crafting beautiful, usable items for myself and others. Investing time and energy in making a pillow, quilt, or scarf seemed like the gift that kept on giving. I took immense pleasure in the process of creation, and I had the joy of using that item or giving it as a gift, knowing that I had put a bit of myself into what I had made.

// the magic was in the act of crafting beautiful, usable items for myself and others //

Traditional Influences, Modern Twist

As I created, I learned from a variety of craft traditions. I pored over books of Amish quilts, African American improvisational quilts, traditional Indian textiles, Seminole Indian patchwork, and the work of the Bauhaus weavers. These explorations led me back to the paintings and design basics I'd learned about in art school. When I began to imagine my own patterns, I sought to integrate these wide-ranging influences into the items I made. I wanted my projects to be rooted in tradition, but to have a modern, fresh twist. I tried varying the scale of a pattern, limiting the palette, employing improvisational piecing techniques, and mixing together different kinds of fabrics.

Project Overview

The projects featured in this book showcase this idea of looking at tradition through a different lens. For example, the Strings Attached Pot Holders and matching Trivet are designed with a nod toward standard string piecing methods, but their energy and freshness come from cutting the strips freehand and trimming the blocks without measuring tools. The same is true for Nate's Quilt, where improvisational cutting and piecing modernize a simplified Log Cabin pattern. Other projects, such as Annie's Picnic Quilt, update basic construction with contemporary fabrics and attention to details. The Honeycomb Hexagon Quilt takes a traditional block and makes it new by increasing the scale, while the Menswear Pillow and Nine-Patch Kitchen Curtain mix different fabrics to take advantage of texture and transparency.

The projects in this book showcase a mix of techniques as well as a range of difficulty levels. Patterns such as the Zigzag Pillow are easy enough for a new sewer, while the Modern Baby Quilt offers a challenge to someone with a few quilts under her belt. The projects are contemporary, useful, and best of all, fun. They're also adaptable. Any one of these quilt patterns can be enlarged or reduced to function as a bed, baby, or wall quilt. Elements from one project can be reconfigured for use in other items. For example, the circular tops from the Round and Round Coasters could be appliquéd to a foundation fabric for a pillow, quilt, or table runner, and the Mix-It-Up Patchwork Scarf piecing pattern could be used for a patchwork skirt or bag. Each of the piecing patterns can be a jumping-off point for other creations.

If in Doubt . . . Wing It!

My best piece of crafting advice came from a wiser and more experienced crafter friend, as I was struggling to understand a pattern, worrying that I hadn't interpreted the instructions properly. I asked for advice, and she said that if I didn't understand the directions, I should just "wing it." At first I thought her response was dismissive, but I came to see it as liberating. She was emancipating me from a slavish devotion to patterns, allowing me to take what I wanted or needed and leave the rest behind.

Now I hope to do the same for you. Re-create the projects as they are pictured or adapt the elements for different purposes. Either way, you'll join in the magic of handmade by putting your stamp on something fresh and contemporary.

An assortment of fabric and thread with dressmaker's shears, pincushion and pins, rotary cutter, quilter's clear acrylic gridded ruler, self-healing cutting mat.

materials + *tools*

→ Every activity has its own set of materials and tools, and sewing is no exception. This chapter introduces you to everything you'll need to make the projects in this book and many more. From fabrics to sewing machines to needles, most sewing essentials are a pleasure to work with, and you'll find yourself collecting fabric, notions, and tools before you know it.

MATERIALS

Materials are the products you use up as you go, such as fabric, batting, and thread. You'll quickly develop a "stash" of leftover fabric scraps and pieces, and yardage that you can't resist buying even if you don't have an immediate project in mind for it. When you see batting or interfacing on sale, it's a good idea to stock up on these, so you're ready when the sewing urge strikes.

Fabric

Sewing requires fabric—lots of it. Fortunately, most people who sew love buying and collecting fabric. All of the projects in this book are made primarily from cotton and linen fabrics. Cotton can run the gamut from translucent organdy to dense corduroy, while linen can be as fine as a handkerchief or rustic and thick. Fabrics made from these fibers are readily available from both online and local fabric stores in many colors and patterns; they're affordable and easy to cut, sew, and wash. I use a variety of different woven cottons in many of the projects, but I avoid cotton knit; it's not suitable for the projects in this book.

Some of the projects in this book are pieced with silk douppioni as well as cotton and linen, for contrast and texture. Silk douppioni is a slightly shiny woven silk with plenty of body, and it comes in a wide range of gorgeous colors. Silk douppioni should be backed with lightweight fusible interfacing when used in quilting projects, because the edges will fray more than with cotton or linen fabric.

Most people who sew quickly accumulate a stash of fabrics and fabric scraps; with my approach to sewing and quilting, a good stash comes in handy and serves as your palette. See Building a Fabric Stash, page 14, for some tips on getting started. Quilt fabric retailers make it easy to stock up by offering fat quarters, cuts of fabric measuring 18" x 22" (45.5 x 56 cm). Collect a variety of fat quarters in colors and prints, and you'll be ready to start on an improvisationally-pieced quilt or project on a moment's notice.

Batting

Batting is the middle layer of the quilt, adding warmth and weight. Batting is available in different fibers and fiber blends and different lofts, or thicknesses.

High-loft batts are made from polyester. I'm not a fan of these because the polyester tends to beard, or work its way through to the fabric surface. Also, I find that the high-loft thickness makes the quilt look more like a comforter than a quilt.

There are many low-loft options in natural fibers, and some are green choices:

→ **Cotton batting** is a good standard batting that's especially suited to quilts for use in warm weather climates. It is available in an organic variety or as a blend with bamboo. Note that cotton batting can shrink noticeably, so plan for shrinkage or follow the manufacturer's instructions for preshrinking the batt.

→ **Bamboo** is a soft, low-loft batting that is easy to work a needle through and so lovely to touch that you'll be reluctant to encase it in the top and backing of your quilt.

→ **Silk** is also a a soft, low-loft batting, although more expensive than cotton or bamboo.

→ **Wool batting** is a perfect low-loft option for a quilt that will be used in colder climates, as well as for a baby quilt, because of the natural water-repellent qualities of wool.

→ **Blended battings** combine the best qualities of two fibers: polyester and cotton, cotton and silk, or cotton and wool.

→ **Heat-resistant batting** combines a layer of reflective metalized film with hollow polyester fibers in a batting designed to reflect energy back to its source.

→ **Fire-retardant batting** is another option for quilts meant for babies or small children. These battings are designed to not melt, flow, or emit toxic fumes when they come into contact with heat or flames. They're often as easy to work with as any other batting and even come in green and/or chemical-free options.

Factor in how closely you're planning to space stitches. If there's too much space between stitches, batting can drift over time and collect in areas of the quilt. Natural-fiber battings typically need to be quilted more closely than polyester battings do. Additionally, needle-punched and bonded battings can tolerate wider spacing of stitches than traditional unbonded battings. Unbonded cotton batting should be stitched every 2" to 3" (5 to 7.5 cm) to prevent shifting,

while a needle-punched cotton or a polyester batting can accommodate stitches that are spaced as much as 8" (20.5 cm) apart. Check the batting package or bolt for the manufacturer's recommendations for quilting distance.

Thread

Look for general-purpose threads for the projects in this book. I consider cotton, polyester, and cotton-wrapped polyester threads to be general-purpose choices.

→ **Cotton thread** comes in a wide range of colors and works with most fabrics except knits and is an excellent choice for quilting. Cotton thread may be labeled for hand or machine quilting, or for both uses. Check that the thread weight is appropriate for the machine, needle, and fabric. Note that some handquilting threads have a waxed finish that is inappropriate for machine sewing.

→ **Polyester thread** is a strong all-purpose sewing thread that's widely available in a vast range of colors; it can be used with most fabrics for hand or machine stitching.

→ **Cotton-wrapped polyester** is an all-purpose thread that's appropriate for knits, wovens, synthetics, and natural fibers. It combines the strength of polyester with the heat resistance of cotton and is a good general sewing thread. Its strength makes it my preferred thread for machine quilting.

If you want to try decorative handstitching, look for six-strand embroidery floss in craft, hobby, and fabric stores. Embroidery floss comes in many colors; use all six strands together or separate the strands and use two or three for a finer detail. An embroidery needle has a large eye to make threading easy.

Interfacing

Interfacing is a product designed to help shape or stiffen fabric. Interfacing comes in a variety of weights and fibers and can be fusible—bonded to the fabric with an iron—or sew-in, attached by stitching to the fabric. In this book, lightweight fusible interfacing is used to back silk douppioni in some of the projects. Fusible interfacing is readily available at fabric and craft stores and comes with manufacturer's instructions for applying.

TOOLS

Tools are the hardware of sewing—the things that you'll use for every project, for pinning, cutting, pressing, and sewing. As with every craft, you'll find that good tools make for good results. Quality sewing tools will last a very long time, so an initial investment will reward you with years of enjoyment and productivity.

Sewing Machine

I love handsewing, and there are several projects in the book that call for some handsewing, but I use a sewing machine for most of my crafts. A good, well-oiled machine is as necessary to sewing as orange juice is to breakfast. You can make any or all of the projects in this book with a basic-model sewing machine; that's what I have, and I sew everything on it. The only requirements are straight and zigzag stitches, a zipper foot, a buttonhole foot (or built-in buttonhole capacity), and feed dogs that can be lowered.

Consistent maintenance is more important than the number of features on your machine. Regular cleaning and oiling and an annual tune-up are essential. Read your owner's manual for information on caring for your machine.

Sewing Machine Needles

Is it really necessary to devote time to explaining sewing machine needles? Yes, because many sewing machine problems can be fixed simply by changing the needle. It's the first thing I do when I'm having a problem. There are many types of sewing machine needles, but the most commonly used are called sharp, ballpoint, and universal needles.

→ **Sharp needles** have a point suited to woven fabrics and are especially useful when sewing straight seams and topstitching. Jeans needles and topstitching needles are also sharp varieties.

→ **Ballpoint needles** are designed to sew knits. The projects in this book don't use knits, but if you do, you'll want to try ballpoint needles.

→ **Universal needles** are appropriate for both woven and knit fabrics.

Needles come in a variety of sizes. The numbers listed on a needle case are associated with two different sizing

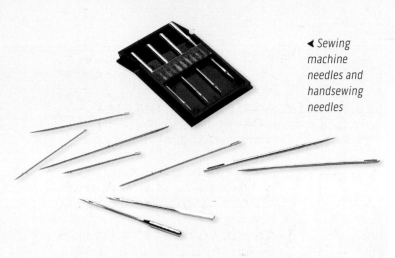

◄ *Sewing machine needles and handsewing needles*

systems. The European method grades needles on a scale from 60 for the finest to 120 for the heaviest. The American system uses a scale of 8 to 19, with 8 being the finest and 19 the heaviest needle. My go-to needle sizes are 80/12 and 90/14. Both sizes sew through cottons and linens well without leaving an unnecessarily large hole. If I were using upholstery fabric, I'd use a heavier needle, and if I were sewing a wedding veil, I'd use a finer needle.

Sewing Machine Feet and Accessories

Sewing machine "feet" are attachments that snap or screw onto the shank of a sewing machine; each is designed for a specific sewing task. For example, a zipper foot is shaped to allow you to stitch close to the zipper teeth.

Sewing machine manufacturers sell feet made to fit their own brand of machines. There are some attachments that claim to fit any brand, but my experience with these so-called universal feet is that they never fit quite right. Most machines come with a few standard attachments, such as a zipper foot and a buttonhole foot, but many more are available.

Some attachments, such as a darning foot or a walking foot, are handy to have and worth the price. A walking foot is especially useful for quilting by machine, because it feeds all the layers of the quilt sandwich evenly. Others, such as a gathering foot, may be superfluous for many sewers, because it's usually possible to gather most fabric using a regular stitch. My almost-daily workhorse attachments are the zipper foot, buttonhole foot, and darning foot. I couldn't create my designs without them.

▲ *Walking foot attachment*

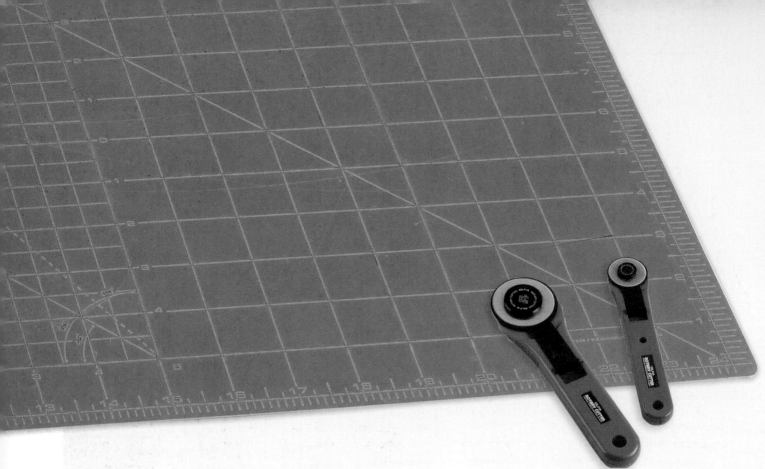

▲ *Self-healing cutting mat and rotary cutters*

For the projects in this book, make sure you have the necessary feet for straight and zigzag stitching and a zipper foot for the pillows and coin purse. A walking foot is not absolutely essential but is very helpful for successful results when machine quilting.

Iron

A good steam iron is so much more than just a wrinkle remover. I use my iron at several points along the way when I'm sewing an item. I press my prewashed fabric. I press the folds out of paper patterns (with a fairly cool dry iron) for accuracy in cutting. I press seams after stitching them. I press the sections of a quilt as I piece them, when I'm preparing the quilt for basting, as I'm turning seams right sides out . . . the list is nearly endless. Pressing as you go can make the difference between a disappointing project and a beautiful, successful one.

I use an iron with a nonstick sole plate, because I find I don't have to clean or worry much about it over time. I also prefer that my iron have steam and spray capabilities, because I use those settings for wrinkled cottons and linens.

Pins

Pins hold paper patterns in place for accurate cutting and hold fabric sections together for ease in sewing. I have two kinds of pins in my studio: medium-size round-head pins and small flat-head pins. I use the round-head pins for general purposes and reserve the flat-head pins for a specific technique called English paper piecing (see page 26).

Rotary Cutter

I use a rotary cutter for just about every cutting job, from slicing strips to cutting around templates to freehand fabric cutting. A rotary cutter is a cutting wheel attached to a handle. Because rotary cutter blades are very sharp, most rotary cutters come with a safety cover to prevent accidents. The blades and their corresponding cutters come in sizes ranging from a diameter of 18 mm to 60 mm. It's handy to have cutters of different sizes; the larger blades can cut through several layers of fabric, and the smaller ones are ideal for cutting around curves.

Self-Healing Cutting Mat

A self-healing cutting mat is essential for cutting with a rotary cutter. Place the mat under your fabric when cutting. On most mats sold for use with rotary cutters for sewing, one side of the mat is gridded and the other is not, but both are appropriate for cutting. Buy a pair of mats in different sizes. Use a large table-size mat to cut out clothing patterns and trim large pieces of fabric and a smaller mat for cutting around templates—you can turn the mat rather than the template as you make your way around. Small mats are portable and perfect

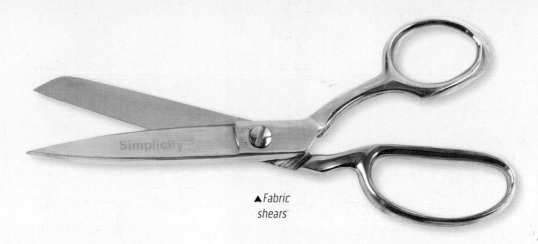

▲Fabric shears

▼Thread clippers

for bringing to classes. Never use a rotary cutter without a mat, because the underlying surface will be damaged, and the blade will quickly dull.

Clear Acrylic Quilter's Ruler

Clear acrylic quilter's rulers with measurement markings come in many sizes; I use a ruler that measures 6" x 24" (15 x 61 cm) to cut full-width strips of 45" (114.5 cm) wide fabric. The grids on the ruler allow for cutting strips in a range of widths and for cutting accurate squares, triangles, and diamonds.

Scissors

I keep scissors handy for a host of tasks, including trimming seam allowances, cutting threads, and clipping curves and corners. Buy scissors that are made for use with fabric; have an inexpensive pair of paper-cutting scissors on hand for other uses. The following types of scissors will be useful as you sew:

➔ **Dressmaker's shears.** I almost always cut fabric with a rotary cutter and cutting mat, but you may wish to have a pair of classic dressmaker's shears if you like to cut fabric with scissors. Choose a good-quality knife-edge pair with 7" (18 cm) or 8" (20.5 cm) blades and bent handles for ease of cutting. Be sure to keep this pair of scissors for fabric only.

➔ **Thread clippers.** These handy little lightweight cutters are nice to have for several tasks, including cutting thread after machine stitching and trimming away thread caught in seam allowances. Many manufacturers make thread clippers that are permanently

attached to mini clips so you can attach the clippers to whatever you're wearing and avoid spending time looking for your clippers.

➔ **Pinking shears.** These specialized scissors feature blades that are saw-toothed and therefore cut in a zigzag pattern rather than straight. They're primarily used for trimming the raw edges of fabric to minimize fraying. Several brands of rotary cutters also offer pinking blades that can be affixed to standard cutter handles. Pinking shears are optional for the projects herein, but you'll find them useful as you expand your sewing repertoire.

Seam Ripper

A seam ripper is a small cutting blade that allows you to quickly and easily remove a row of stitching without tearing or stretching the fabric. Unless you're planning on never making a mistake or changing your mind mid-project, make sure that your sewing kit includes a seam ripper. I have dozens of them tucked into various corners of my studio. They're inexpensive tools, so buy a few.

Point Turner

A point turner is a device made for pushing out corners of sewn items. After sewing a bag or pillow, for example, and turning it right side out, you'll want to gently push the fabric in the corners all the way out for a smooth, flat edge. A point turner is pointed but blunt, so it won't poke through your stitching. You can also carefully use a knitting needle or pencil to turn corners, but don't be tempted to use sharp scissors—you'll risk going all the way through the fabric.

▲Seam ripper

building a fabric stash

You don't have to sew for very long before you find yourself with a fabric "stash." For many sewists, the size of their stash is limited only by how much storage room they have, as they collect scraps, found fabrics, and fabrics purchased without a particular project in mind. For my style of improvisational, fearlessly colorful quilting, a healthy stash is like a painter's palette—a part of your artistic toolbox that allows you free expression.

How do you start a stash? Begin by saving scraps and leftover short pieces from your projects and add purchased fabrics whenever you see a fabric that you love, or something in an unusual color, or when a sale will save you some money. In addition to buying from local fabric stores, you can order fabric from practically any store in the world via the Internet or telephone. Many online fabric vendors offer wonderful specialty fabrics; for example, Etsy.com, a popular online marketplace, is a good place to find Japanese, African, and vintage fabrics.

If you like to buy local, don't limit yourself to fabric stores. Thrift or secondhand stores are full of fabric treasures. Closely inspect any used garment or textile you purchase to determine how much of the fabric is usable. Another unsung fabric source is the linen section of your local department store. A 100 percent cotton, twin-size flat sheet measures about 66" × 96" (167.5 × 244 cm), almost 4 yards (3.6 m) of fabric. If you like the color or print, who's to know that the feature fabric of your bag started life as a bedsheet?

When I purchase fabric, I try to buy at least 1 yard (91.5 cm) if I plan to use it in patchwork and 3 yards (2.7 m) if I intend to use the fabric for clothing. I prefer to have extra rather than not enough, but when it comes to building a stash, even a fat quarter or half yard will find a home. I follow my gut instinct; if I'm drawn to a fabric, I try to trust that and, barring excessive cost, buy some!

Needles for Sewing by Hand

There are many kinds of handsewing needles intended for different uses. For cotton and linen fabrics, the most commonly used needles are sharps, embroidery needles, and quilting needles (also called betweens).

→ **Sharps.** The most commonly used needle are sharps, and as the name implies, they are sharp. They are medium-size when compared to the small betweens and long milliner needles and have a rounded eye just large enough to fit the thread. They're sized from 1 to 10 based on diameter, with 1 the thickest and 10 the thinnest. Use the needle that makes the smallest hole as it passes through the fabric while still spreading the fibers enough for the thread to pass through.

→ **Embroidery needles.** Though similar to sharps, embroidery or crewel needles have larger eyes to accommodate embroidery threads.

→ **Quilting/Betweens.** Quilting needles, or betweens, are sharp and thin, ideal for handquilting. They have small eyes like sharps and come in a range of sizes. Betweens are shorter than sharps; their lengths do vary. However, their thickness varies, too, with larger numbers indicating smaller diameter. If you've never handquilted, start with a larger needle and gradually move to smaller sizes as you get comfortable.

There are a few specialty needles that are worth mentioning. Tapestry needles have a blunt point and a large eye and are great for stitching with yarn or tying quilts when the fabric is loosely woven enough to allow the blunt point to penetrate the fabric layers. Chenilles also have a large eye but a sharper point; these work well for ribbon embroidery as well as standard embroidery.

Fabric Marking Tools

I use fabric marking tools to transfer pattern information and to mark quilting designs. Choose one that will vanish in a few hours with exposure to air or a water-soluble one that can be washed away with water. There are many types of fabric pens and pencils, but all are meant to only temporarily mark fabric. Always test the pen or pencil on a discreet part of the fabric to make sure the mark is washable or fades. Even when using an air-soluble or a vanishing marker, it's a good idea to remove the marks thoroughly with plenty of water to ensure they won't reappear at a later date. If the fabric is nonwashable, chalk may be a better marking choice.

Quilt Basting Tools

For quilt basting, I use curved safety pins, a Kwik Klip tool to aid in closing the pins, and masking tape. In the project instructions in this book, this group of tools is referred to as quilt basting tools.

→ **Plain masking tape**, available at any grocery store, allows you to temporarily adhere the quilt backing to a flat surface while basting. Masking tape will not leave a sticky residue on your floor or fabric.

→ **Quilter's curved safety pins**, about 1½" (3.8 cm) long, are ideal for temporarily holding the quilt layers together during quilting. I usually buy these in large boxes because it's better to have too many than not enough.

→ A **quilter's safety-pin fastening tool**, such as a Kwik Klip tool, may seem like an unnecessary gadget, but if you've ever basted a large quilt and had blistered fingers from closing safety pins, you'll recognize the advantages of using this tool. It is a thin, short metal wand attached to a wooden handle that slips underneath the open safety pin and helps you close the pin.

Quilting Frames and Hoops

Quilting frames and hoops make handquilting easy, help prevent puckering, and aid in making even stitches. Available in several styles and sizes, from small handheld quilting hoops to room-size frames, they all work by allowing you to stretch the quilt sandwich taut for ease of stitching. Quilting frames are four-sided, often self-supporting, and can be quite large. They're great for large quilts and allow multiple quilters to work simultaneously. Quilting hoops are round or oval and consist of two pieces, one slightly smaller than the other. The smaller piece fits inside the larger one, with the quilt in between, and a butterfly screw lets you tighten the tension. Quilting hoops differ from embroidery hoops in that they have deeper sides to support the multiple layers of a quilt.

basic sewing tool kit

Most of the tools in this chapter are necessary for each project in this book; consider these items your basic sewing tool kit that will allow you to make almost anything. Any optional or additional tools for a specific project are listed with the instructions for that project.

→ Sewing machine capable of straight and zigzag stitching with zipper foot attachment and walking foot attachment

→ Steam iron

→ Pins

→ Sewing machine needles

→ Handsewing needles

→ Straight pins

→ Fabric scissors

→ Thread clippers

→ Seam ripper

→ Point turner

→ Rotary cutter

→ Self-healing cutting mat

→ Quilter's clear acrylic rulers

→ Disappearing fabric marking pen

→ Quilter's curved safety pins for pin basting

essential *techniques*
for patchwork, quilting + finishing

→ The art of piecing fabrics together, layering them, and securing them with visible stitching—patchwork and quilting—goes back hundreds of years, long before rotary cutters or even sewing machines were invented. My approach to quilting makes the most of modern tools and contemporary fabrics to create designs that are fun and functional. I use the basic piecing, basting, quilting, binding, and finishing techniques described in this chapter every day, and they'll serve you well for the projects that follow and beyond.

PREPARING TO SEW

A little preparation goes a long way when you're piecing and quilting. Pretreating fabric, careful cutting with good-quality tools, and straightening the grain of your fabric, all before you take a single stitch, will help guarantee beautiful results.

Preparing Fabric

I always machine wash, machine dry, and press all my cotton and linen fabric before cutting and sewing. Silk douppioni can also be washed and dried by machine, but it will change the hand of the fabric considerably, from crisp to soft, and colors may run, so wash silk separately.

Prewashing and drying fabric ensures that any shrinkage happens before you make your project, so it won't be ruined by excessive shrinkage the first time you wash it. Pressing the fabric before cutting makes for greater accuracy. These steps take only a little extra time but will help you get professional results.

Going with (or against) the Grain

Before you cut your fabric, you need an understanding of grain; just as wood has a grain, so does fabric, and the way a pattern piece or template is placed relative to the grain affects the way that the cut fabric will behave and drape. Grain markings on pattern templates indicate how to align the template to the selvedge *(fig. 1, page 18)*. By understanding the three types of fabric grain, you can cut your fabric to work with you, not against you. For example, binding cut on the bias grain will go easily around curves on a shaped quilt.

The lengthwise grain is comprised of the warp threads, indicated by the selvedge, or firm woven edge of the fabric. Pattern pieces placed parallel to the selvedge are said to be cut on the lengthwise grain. These pieces have the most strength and stability.

The crosswise grain (or cross grain) consists of the weft threads, or the threads that run from selvedge to selvedge. Pattern pieces aligned this way, with the grainline on the pattern piece perpendicular to the selvedge, are cut

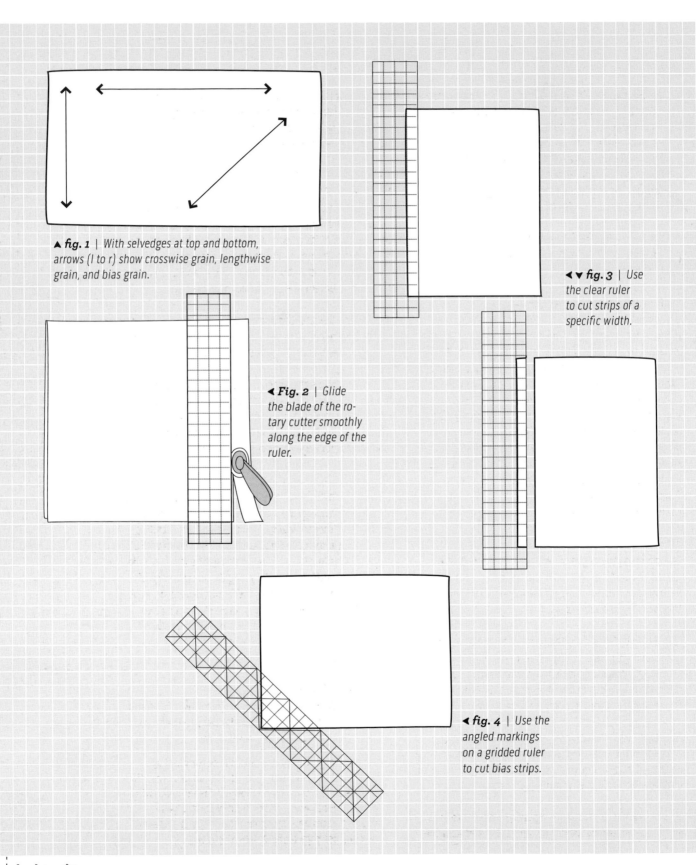

▲ *fig. 1* | *With selvedges at top and bottom, arrows (l to r) show crosswise grain, lengthwise grain, and bias grain.*

◄ **Fig. 2** | *Glide the blade of the rotary cutter smoothly along the edge of the ruler.*

◄ ▼ *fig. 3* | *Use the clear ruler to cut strips of a specific width.*

◄ *fig. 4* | *Use the angled markings on a gridded ruler to cut bias strips.*

on the crosswise grain. The crosswise grain may have a little bit of stretch to it; though stable, it is not as stable as the lengthwise grain. Both lengthwise and crosswise grains may also be referred to as straight grain.

The bias grain is at a 45° angle to the lengthwise and crosswise grain (in other words, the bias is the diagonal of the fabric). The bias grain is less stable than the straight grain, and a piece cut with this orientation will stretch.

Using a Rotary Cutter, Cutting Mat, and Clear Acrylic Ruler

I almost always use a rotary cutter, together with a self-healing cutting mat, to cut my fabric, even when trimming fabric or cutting an intricate shape for appliqué. When cutting rectangles, squares, or strips of fabric for piecing or binding, I use a clear acrylic ruler with markings, often called a quilter's ruler, with my rotary cutter and mat.

To use a rotary cutter safely, some general principles apply. Always close the blade of your cutter with the safety cover when it's not in use. The safety cover should be engaged at any moment when you're not actually cutting fabric. If you're cutting strips and need to reposition the fabric, close the cutter while making adjustments. You should never, ever reach for a rotary cutter and find the blade uncovered. Second, use your nondominant hand, fingers spread apart, to steady the ruler when using it in conjunction with a rotary cutter.

Truing Up Fabric

Straightening the edges of fabric and ensuring that the lengthwise and crosswise threads are "on grain" at 90° to each other, is called truing up the fabric. It's a helpful step that will improve your results.

1 | Begin by folding the fabric along the lengthwise grain, laying the selvedges precisely on top of one another. The fold becomes a guide for placing the edge of a quilter's clear acrylic ruler. Abut the short edge of the ruler to the folded line; with your nondominant hand, steady the ruler.

2 | Open your rotary cutter and glide the blade along the edge of the ruler (*fig. 2*). Your newly cut line is now a perfectly straight edge and can function as a guideline for cutting strips or further trimming your fabric.

3 | If you'd like to trim the edge perpendicular to your straight edge, simply rotate your fabric 90° and abut the

short edge of the ruler along the straightened edge; cut a straight edge perpendicular to your first cut edge. At this point you'll have a fold plus two straightened edges to use as a reference for cutting.

Cutting Strips on the Lengthwise or Crosswise Grain

Cutting strips on the lengthwise or crosswise grain is as basic to quilting as buttering and flouring a pan is to baking. Luckily, it's as easy as prepping a baking dish, and there's little chance of getting flour on your shirt. First, follow Steps 1 and 2 above to true up the fabric. You now have a cut straight line and a folded straight line.

1 | Rotate the fabric or the cutting mat so that the fabric can be further cut along either the left or the right side of your ruler, depending on your dominant hand.

2 | To cut strips of a specific width, align the vertical mark on the ruler that corresponds to your desired width with the cut straight edge of the fabric. Steady the ruler with your nondominant hand and glide the rotary blade along the outer edge of the ruler (*fig. 3*).

Cutting Bias Strips

Because the bias grain (diagonal to the selvedge) stretches, binding strips cut on the bias can smoothly cover rounded or unusually shaped edges. Use your rotary cutter, cutting mat, and clear ruler combo to cut bias strips. Begin with a piece of fabric that has at least one straight edge. Place the 45° line indicated on the ruler along the straight edge of the fabric and cut a line across the fabric (*fig. 4*). This cut edge will now function as your guideline for cutting bias strips. For example, to cut 1½" (3.8 cm) wide bias strips, align that marking on your ruler with the newly cut edge and cut along the long edge of the ruler.

Using Templates

This book includes several templates (patterns) at the back of the book to allow you to accurately re-create the pictured projects. Some tips for using these patterns:

→ Reproduce the templates and, if necessary, enlarge them to the correct size. Copy the templates onto stiff paper such as card stock, enlarging the template with a copier or scanner and printer if needed. If you're copying a template multiple times for English paper piecing, use copy paper or freezer paper.

→ Be sure to press your fabric before placing the template on the fabric and cutting. It's often helpful, especially with linen, to apply a bit of spray starch to the fabric.

→ When you've readied the fabric, place the fabric right side up on your self-healing cutting mat, then place the template right side up on the fabric.

→ Steady the template with your nondominant hand and use a small-bladed rotary cutter to cut around the outline of the template. Be careful not to cut the template. If the template is a simple shape with straight edges, you can use a larger rotary blade to cut through several layers of fabric at once.

→ To cut complex shapes that require turning to cut around the entire shape, I prefer to use a small mat because I can rotate the mat to ease the cutting rather than moving the template.

→ You can also trace around the template with a pencil or fabric marker and then cut the shape with dressmaker's shears. Make sure the marks are removable, or turn both the template and the fabric wrong side up and mark on the fabric wrong side.

Understanding Seam Allowance

Seam allowance is the distance between the raw edge of your fabric (the cutting line) and the stitching line *(fig. 5)*. The seam allowance determines how much additional fabric you'll need on a piece of fabric to achieve the desired end result. For example, if you want a 4" (10 cm) square on your finished quilt, and you're using a ¼" (6 mm) seam allowance, you'll need to add ¼" (6 mm) to all sides of the square, cutting a 4½" x 4½" (11.5 x 11.5 cm) piece of fabric.

Traditionally, quilt tops are pieced using a ¼" (6 mm) seam allowance while garments are sewn using a ⅝" (1.5 cm), ½" (1.3 cm), or ³/₈" (1 cm) seam allowance. Most sewing machines will have grooves along the faceplate to indicate these measurements *(fig. 6)*. The ¼" (6 mm) point, relative to the needle, often falls along the right edge of the presser foot. If you're not sure whether that's true for your machine, measure a distance of ¼" (6 mm) to the right of your needle and mark that

line with a bit of masking tape. This will guarantee you consistent results when machine piecing.

Ripping a Seam

Everyone makes mistakes, and in sewing, ripping a seam is akin to erasing an unwanted mark. This technique allows you to remove long lines of stitching without having to cut through each stitch individually. With a line of stitching facing you, use the seam ripper to pick up and slice through every third or fourth stitch across the entire line of stitching, being careful not to clip a fabric thread. Turn the stitching to the "unsliced" side and gently tug on the thread. You should be able to remove long sections of thread and separate the previously sewn pieces.

Pressing Seams

Quilters differ on the best way to treat seams in patchwork. One philosophy calls for all seams to be pressed open, while others advocate pressing seams to one side. My noncommittal response to this issue is to say, "It depends." It depends on the project, and each set of project instructions in this book includes my pressing preferences for that specific item.

A few tips on technique: although it's called an iron, don't iron seams. Ironing is for wrinkled bed sheets. Gently press the seam, moving the iron up and down with a smooth, steady motion. Whether pressing the seam open or to the side, run your finger along the seam before applying the iron to establish the seam.

MACHINE STITCHING

Depending on the make and model of your sewing machine, you may have anywhere from just a few stitch options to more choices than Imelda Marcos had shoes. Most modern machines have at least a straight, zigzag, and satin stitch (a very close zigzag stitch), and these three stitches *(fig. 7)* will allow you to make all of the projects in this book and many more.

Straight stitches are workhorse stitches, perfect for securing seams. Almost all of my sewing is done with my machine needle set for straight stitch. Most machines give you a choice of stitch lengths and widths; for straight stitch, only stitch length applies. Set your stitch length for 10 to 12 stitches per 1" (2.5 cm).

▲ **fig. 5** | Dotted line indicates seamline or stitching line; solid line indicates cutting line.

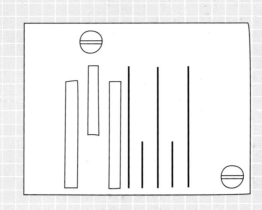

◄ **fig. 6** | The throat plate of your sewing machine has measurements to the right of the needle (shown as heavy solid lines) to help measure seam allowances.

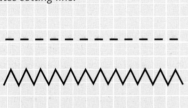

▲ **fig. 7** | From top, straight stitch, zigzag stitch, and satin stitch.

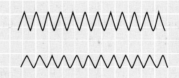

▼ **fig. 8** | Use a smaller straight stitch for seams (top) and a longer one for basting.

◄ **fig. 9** | Variations of zigzag stitch made by adjusting stitch length and width.

On most machines, setting the stitch length to a lower number creates smaller stitches, while a higher number yields larger stitches. Newer machines calibrate stitch length in millimeters (mm), and a normal stitch length of 2.5 mm corresponds to ten stitches per 1" (2.5 cm).

Most of my stitching is done at the 2.5 mm setting on my machine. This creates a line of stitches that are close enough to hold fabric securely and not so close that they're impossible to rip apart if needed.

However, other settings have a purpose. A stitch length setting of 4 or 5 mm on my machine is ideal for basting or for gathering fabric. These stitches are substantially larger and easier to remove or manipulate than the smaller stitches used for piecing and quilting **(fig. 8)**.

Zigzag Stitch

Zigzag stitches are also wonderful for securing fabric, but because of their unique shape; they're not appropriate for sewing simple seams. Zigzag stitching works well as a secure topstitch for bindings and hems and can be decorative as well as functional. You can adjust the stitch width as well as the length for zigzag stitches **(fig. 9)**.

Satin Stitch

A machine set to zigzag at a very small stitch length creates tightly packed zigzags, or satin stitch. This stitch is used for machine appliquéing, to secure and cover a raw edge, and for buttonholes. Like standard

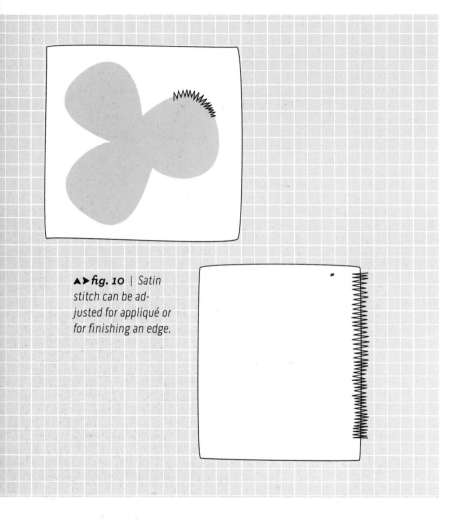

▲▶ *fig. 10* | *Satin stitch can be adjusted for appliqué or for finishing an edge.*

zigzag stitch, satin stitch can be both attractive and useful. By adjusting stitch width, you can get a narrow or bold line of satin stitch *(fig. 10)*. When setting the stitch length for satin stitches, always test the stitch on a fabric scrap to ensure that the stitches lie close enough together for full coverage without bunching up or distorting the fabric.

Topstitching

Topstitching is a decorative stitch—usually a straight stitch—applied to the outside of an item for decorative purposes, usually sewn close to an edge to accent that edge. Because topstitching is meant to be seen, your seams, whether pressed open or to one side, should be thoroughly pressed to lie as flat as possible before adding the accent stitches. Use your machine presser foot to help guide your topstitching.

HANDSTITCHING

Learning to skillfully execute a few simple stitches by hand will help you create beautifully finished quilts and garments. Many sewers find it relaxing and enjoyable to stitch by hand. Try running your length of thread through a cake of beeswax, sold with sewing notions at craft and fabric stores, to keep it from tangling.

Basting

Basting means sewing pieces of fabric together temporarily with easily removed stitches to hold them in place before final stitching. When I layer a quilt top, batting, and backing, I pin-baste using quilter's curved safety pins, but hand-basting with needle and thread is a useful technique in many sewing projects. Simply thread a handsewing needle, knot the end of the thread, and make long stitches as needed, not too tightly; the layers should be held in place without shifting, but still lie flat. After you've done your final hand or machine stitching, clip the basting thread and pull it out. If you baste with a contrasting-color thread, it's easy to see when you're ready to remove it.

Slip Stitch

Slip stitching *(fig. 11, page 23)* is a handsewing technique that allows you to join a folded edge and a flat piece of fabric in a way that's nearly invisible. It's suitable when hand-finishing quilt bindings, stitching an appliqué, or attaching a hem to a garment. To slip-stitch:

1 | Thread the needle with a single strand of thread and knot the thread tail. Pull the needle and thread through the folded edge from the wrong side, so the knot is hidden inside the fold.

2 | Take a tiny stitch into the flat fabric, picking up only one or two fabric threads, then pull the thread snug (but not too tight).

3 | Slip the needle back inside the first fabric fold where it emerged and glide through the fold for about ¼" (6 mm) before coming out of the fold to make the next stitch.

Ladder Stitch

Ladder stitch *(fig. 12)* is most often used for stitching two folded edges together, as when closing openings on items you've turned right side out. Pressing is essential; be sure to iron the folded edges flat for a nice crisp edge that's easy to work with.

1 | After threading a needle and knotting the thread, insert needle into folded edge and pull both needle and thread through.

2 | Slip needle through opposite folded edge for about ¼" (6 mm), being sure to draw the needle and thread completely through.

3 | Continue slipping the needle through opposite edges until the opening has been sewn closed. Knot and clip the thread.

Running Stitch

The running stitch *(fig. 13)* is the simplest of stitches. Spaced closely and evenly, it's the handquilting stitch; spaced long and loose, it's a basting stitch. The running stitch can also be a decorative element; try a line or three of running stitch made with embroidery floss to dress up a simple project.

1 | Bring the needle up from beneath the fabric.

2 | Bring the needle back down into the fabric about ⅛" to ¼" (3 mm to 6 mm) from the starting point.

3 | Bring the needle up to the left, spacing stitches evenly.

As you gain skill, you can insert and bring up the needle several times before pulling the thread through, and you'll begin to develop a graceful and comfortable rhythm.

Blanket Stitch

Blanket stitch *(fig. 14)* is a decorative embroidery stitch that I use for appliqué, such as on the Flower Garden Sham, page 47. It's easy to learn and practice.

1 | Working from left to right, bring the needle up at point 1 and insert at point 2.

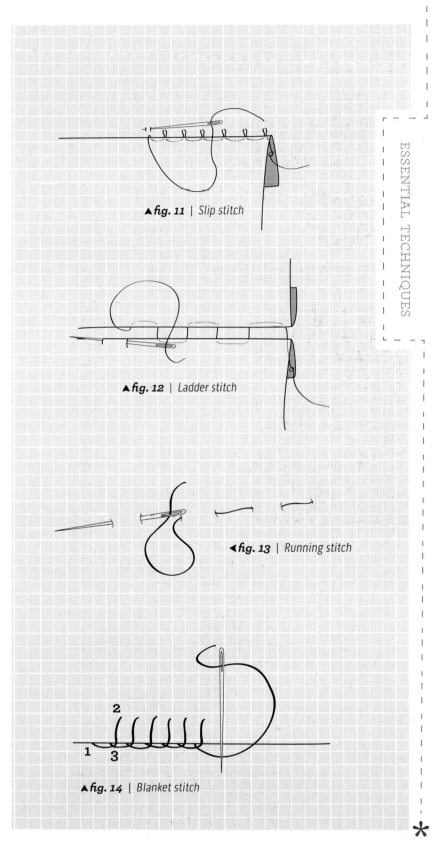

▲ *fig. 11* | Slip stitch

▲ *fig. 12* | Ladder stitch

◄ *fig. 13* | Running stitch

▲ *fig. 14* | Blanket stitch

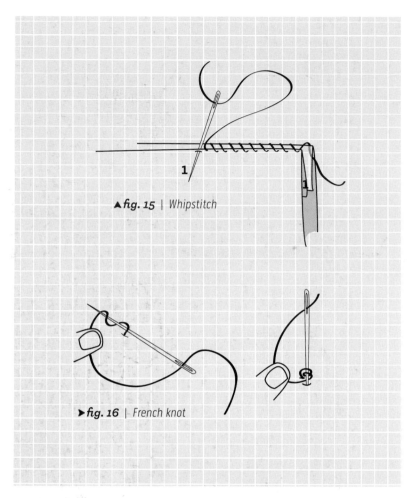

▲ *fig. 15* | *Whipstitch*

▶ *fig. 16* | *French knot*

▶ *A classic
nine-patch
block becomes
contemporary in
Japanese fabrics
surrounded by
sheer bands
(project,
page 85).*

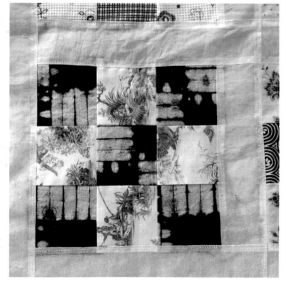

2 | Bring the needle back up at point 3 and over
the working thread. Repeat.

Blanket stitch is terrific for securing an appliqué to
foundation fabric; just make sure that the bottoms of the
stitches line up with the edge of the appliqué.

Whipstitch

Whipstitch *(fig. 15)* stitches can be finely spaced or, for a
more decorative look, placed farther apart.

1 | Secure the thread inside the fold and bring the
needle through both folds to emerge on the front fabric.

2 | Pass the needle over the fabric edges, then insert it
through both fabric layers.

3 | Repeat the process of passing the thread over the
fabric edges and through the fabric layers.

French Knot

French knot *(fig. 16)* is a decorative knot worked on the
fabric surface to add texture or provide details, such as
eyes. French knots are often used in multiples.

1 | Bring the needle up at point 1 and hold the thread
taut about 2" (5 cm) above the fabric.

2 | Point the needle toward your fingers and wrap the
thread tautly around the needle twice.

3 | Insert the needle into the fabric near point 1 and
complete the knot by holding the thread taut near the
wrapped thread as you pull the needle through the wraps
and fabric.

PIECING THE QUILT TOP

I love the word patchwork and the way it refers to assem-
bling something out of many possibly disparate pieces.
There are several approaches to piecing a quilt top; the
shape of the fabric to be pieced determines the best choice.
For example, chain piecing is perfect for a series of same-
size squares, while a freehand curved piecing technique
suits curves cut improvisationally. This section details these
and other techniques for sewing patches into patchwork.

Chain Piecing

I liken chain piecing to having an electric garage door opener—it's not essential, but it's so amazingly handy. Chain piecing allows you to machine sew multiples of the same shape without cutting your thread.

To chain piece a stack of same-size squares:

1 | Place two squares right sides together.

2 | Beginning with the first pair, machine stitch the squares together, maintaining a ¼" (6 mm) seam allowance.

3 | Once the first pair of squares has passed underneath the presser foot, sew a couple of extra stitches while gently holding the seamed squares. This creates a small chain of stitches separating the first pair of squares from the next. Do not cut the thread.

4 | Position a second pair of squares under the presser foot and stitch. As in the first pair, continue stitching past the edge of the fabric. Repeat this process until all the squares are stitched into pairs.

5 | Use thread snippers or scissors to snip the pairs apart, as shown in **fig. 17**.

Y Piecing

Why the Y? Because this technique allows you to sew together an intersection of seams that form a Y. These types of seams are often sewn by hand, but with a little care and backstitching you can sew them up in a fraction of the time on a sewing machine. **Fig. 18** illustrates the following steps.

1 | Begin by aligning the outside and central corners of two pieces, right sides together. Pin and stitch from the outside corner to the central corner, stopping ¼" (6 mm) short of the central corner (at the point where the seamlines intersect). Backstitch to secure the seam.

2 | Align one outside corner and the central corner of a third piece with the sewn pair, right sides together. Make sure the seam allowance of the first seam lies to one side so it is not caught in the new seam.

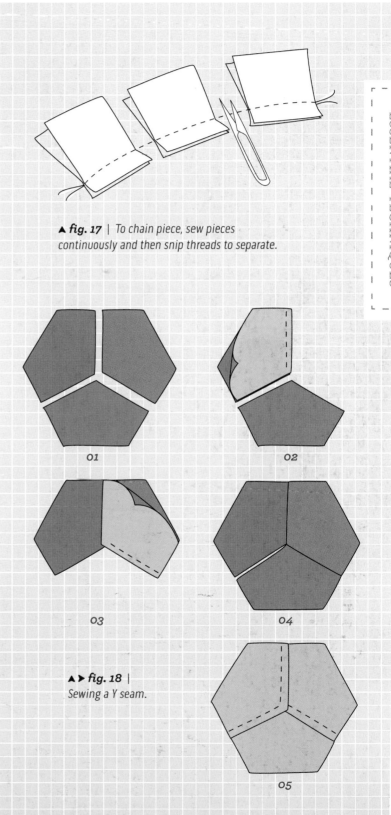

▲ **fig. 17** | *To chain piece, sew pieces continuously and then snip threads to separate.*

01

02

03

04

▲▶ **fig. 18** |
Sewing a Y seam.

05

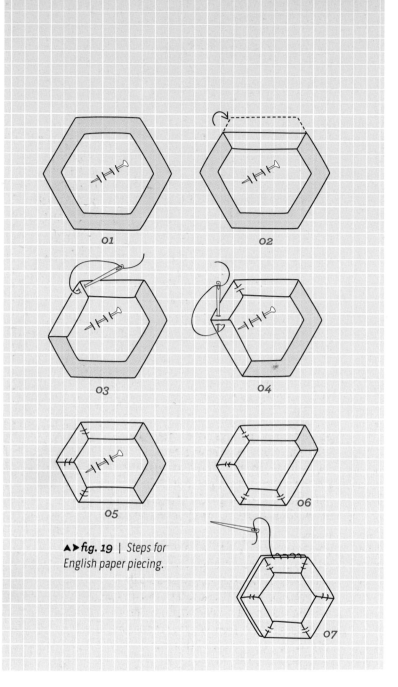

01   02   03   04   05   06   07

▲▶ *fig. 19* | *Steps for English paper piecing.*

for sewing intricate patterns with a lot of matched points. The patterns are based on a single patch shape, usually diamonds, triangles, or hexagons. Piecing these shapes can be accomplished on a machine using Y seams; however, the technique that follows allows you to build a quilt top in modules and is completely portable. *Fig. 19* illustrates the steps for English paper piecing with a hexagon-shaped module. Start by cutting multiple templates out of paper—you'll need one paper shape for each individual patch. Copy the templates onto plain white copy paper or freezer paper.

1 | Place the fabric wrong side up on a hard surface. Secure each paper template with a pin allowing at least ½" (1.3 cm) between templates. I use pins with small flat heads, because they don't interfere with the sewing. (If using freezer paper templates, just use a dry, warm iron to press the shiny side of the freezer paper shape to the wrong side of the fabric.)

2 | Spray starch into a small bowl and apply with a small brush or your fingertip to the seam allowances only, avoiding the paper templates, and press the seam allowances over the template edges.

3 | On the wrong side, hand-baste the seam allowance corners, being sure not to catch the paper in the stitching. Sew the patches right sides together. Whipstitch is most often used, but you can also use a closely spaced ladder stitch or a slip stitch, picking up only two or three fabric threads with each stitch. The patches are sewn together in pairs; reposition them as needed to ensure they lie flat and are always sewn right sides together. When the patchwork is complete, remove the paper templates and press the patchwork again.

Improvisational Piecing

Piecing improvisationally is more about mind-set than it is about actual technique, but there are some concrete ideas to keep in mind when working this way. Most important: put your measuring tools away. Cut strips, squares, triangles, and other shapes with just a rotary cutter and self-healing mat. Trust your eye and you'll be amazed at how accurate you are.

Be willing to add, delete, and trim parts of a block to make it fit with an adjoining block or section. When I'm piecing together two differently shaped or sized fabrics that are placed right sides together, I designate the outer

3 | Pin and stitch from the outside corner to the central corner, stopping ¼" (6 mm) short of the central corner and backstitching. The two seams will end at the same point.

4 | Match the central and outside corners of the first and last patches to sew the remaining seam. Pin and stitch, starting ¼" (6 mm) in from the central corner and sewing to the outside corner. The Y seam is complete.

English Paper Piecing

English paper piecing is about as traditional as it gets, dating back to at least 1813. It's a handstitching method edge of the top piece as my straight edge. This gives me an edge to position under my presser foot for my ¼" (6 mm) seam allowance. See more tips on improvisational piecing in the sidebar on page 131.

Squaring a Block Made with Improvisational Piecing

Squaring a block is especially useful when using the improvisational piecing method. This free-form method of piecing yields raw, energetic blocks, but variations in size can make it difficult to stitch larger sections together. Squaring resolves these variations. You can square parts of a quilt top at any point as you're piecing the top; you might square every block as you make it or piece together several blocks and then square the larger section.

1 | Begin by folding the block or section in half. Finger-press to establish the fold, which will temporarily function as a straight edge and provide a guideline for additional cuts.

2 | Position a clear acrylic ruler with one of its short lines along the fabric crease and the ruler's long edge near a fabric raw edge. Trim the fabric along the long edge of the ruler. The aim is to create a perfectly straight edge perpendicular to the fold without cutting away too much of the patchwork.

3 | Unfold the fabric and reposition the short edge of the ruler along the newly cut straight edge, near one end. Trim a little of the patchwork to create a second straight edge perpendicular to the first. Repeat to straighten the other two edges.

4 | To cut a block or section to a specific size, first trim to create straight edges and then measure and cut to size.

Appliqué

Appliqué means to sew one piece of fabric by hand or machine onto a foundation piece. Appliqué is an ideal technique for shapes that would be difficult to piece, such as circles, free-form shapes, or letters.

To appliqué by hand:
1 | Cut the shape to be applied, adding a seam allowance of about ¼" (6 mm) all around; you'll turn under this raw edge.

◄ Nate's Quilt (page 127) makes the most of improvisational piecing and bold color choices.

2 | If desired, stitch around the edge of the shape on the stitching line (not the cutting line). Clip into the seam allowance, clipping to but not through the stitching on the stitching line **(fig. 20)**. Space the clips ¼" to ½" (6 mm to 1.3 cm) apart, depending on the appliqué's size; smaller appliqués and tighter curves need more closely spaced clips.

3 | In preparation for stitching the applied shape, sandwich the foundation fabric in an embroidery hoop to keep it taut during stitching. Pin the applied shape to the foundation fabric. Fold under the clipped seam allowance (if you machine stitched around the stitching line of the shape, make sure the stitching is turned under) and begin to slip-stitch the folded edge to the foundation fabric; continue to turn under as you go.

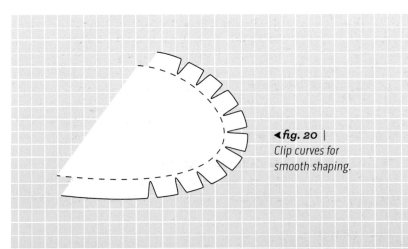

◄ **fig. 20** |
Clip curves for smooth shaping.

To appliqué by machine:

1 | Cut the shape to its final measurements. You do not need to add a seam allowance for machine-appliquéd shapes.

2 | Pin the shape to the foundation fabric and use a machine satin stitch (a zigzag stitch with a very short stitch length [usually 0.3 to 0.4 mm], so the stitches are close together; see page 22) to encase the raw edge. Satin stitch slowly all around the shape, positioning the presser foot so the left swing of the needle falls in the appliqué shape and the right swing enters only the foundation fabric just beyond the appliqué edge. Pivot frequently as you go to keep the shape positioned properly.

PREPARING FOR QUILTING

A quilt is not really a quilt until it has batting and a backing. Adding these layers gives the pieced top texture and warmth and makes the quilt truly functional. Once you've finished the quilt top, you're ready to assemble the three layers and begin quilting to hold the layers together.

Estimating Batting and Backing Amounts

Choose backing fabric that's about the same weight as the quilt top. I recommend 100 percent cotton fabric. Avoid anything stretchy.

Backing fabric should measure at least 8" (20.5 cm) wider and 8" (20.5 cm) longer than the quilt top. Most quilting fabrics come in 45" (114.5 cm) widths but may

have only 42" (106.5 cm) of useable fabric between the selvedges, so if a quilt top is more than 35" (89 cm) wide, piece the backing fabric. If possible, the lengthwise grain of the backing fabric should run parallel to the length of the quilt because there's less stretch along that grain.

For example, if a quilt top is 60" x 80" (152.5 x 203 cm), the backing should measure at least 68" x 88" (173 x 223.5 cm). From 4 yards (3.7 m) of 45" (114.5 cm) wide fabric, cut two pieces each measuring 36" x 90" (91.5 x 229 cm). Stitch the two pieces, right sides together, along the 90" (229 cm) edges to create a backing piece a bit larger than the minimum requirements. As a general guide, these yardages will be adequate to piece backing for standard bed-size quilts from 45" (114.5 cm) wide fabric:

Twin	5¼ yd (4.8 m)
Double	5¼ yd (4.8 m)
Queen	7½ yd (6.9 m)
King	8¼ yd (7.5 m)

It's possible to purchase fabric sized to function as quilt backing without piecing. Many quilt shops sell fabrics measuring up to 110" (2.8 m) wide. The selection is limited but growing, and if you'd prefer to avoid any seams in the backing, this option is worth considering.

I usually craft my backings exclusively out of one fabric. That is, I don't piece the backing any more than is necessary to create a length of fabric large enough to serve as backing. Some quilters like to incorporate elements of the quilt top design in the backing and add patchwork there as well. Oftentimes the patchwork is limited to a strip of blocks or several coordinating fabrics. Be aware that additional seams in the backing can make quilting, particularly handquilting, difficult.

Batting should also be cut larger than the quilt top in all directions. If you buy batting by the yard or meter, take into consideration the length of your top and make sure the batting is at least 8" (20 cm) longer. Batting is also sold in precut packages for standard bed sizes.

Pin-Basting a Quilt

You've pieced a quilt top, stood back, and admired your creation—now it's time to tackle the actual quilting. You can tie, handquilt, or machine quilt the layers that make up your quilt, but you're going to have to baste them together first. Basting a quilt temporarily holds the layers together during finishing, and keeps the layers from shifting as you quilt.

▶ *This detail of the Modern Baby Quilt (page 117) shows quilting, piecing with hexagons, and binding.*

Although basting traditionally refers to large stitches with a needle and thread, I find it faster and easier to "baste" my quilts and quilted projects with safety pins—curved safety pins made especially for quilters—as follows:

1 | On a flat, firm surface such as a tabletop or floor, lay down the backing fabric, wrong side up. Working from the center out, smooth fabric and secure to the surface with masking tape. The fabric should be taut and wrinkle free, but not stretched.

2 | Layer batting and quilt top, right side up, on top of backing. Smooth the batting and quilt top from the center out to eliminate wrinkles.

3 | Beginning in the center of the quilt top, pin safety pins about every 4" (10 cm) through all three layers. Work in concentric circles, either clockwise or counterclockwise, until the entire top is securely pinned to other layers.

4 | If you're working with a large quilt, closing safety pins can tire your hands. If you like, look for a special tool for fastening curved safety pins, such as Kwik Klip, at your quilt or fabric store.

5 | Remove the masking tape and your quilt is ready to be tied or quilted.

QUILTING

Technically speaking, patchwork is a textile made of different fabrics pieced together. A quilt is a layered textile with a top fabric, often made of patchwork; a middle layer, usually a batting of cotton or wool; and a backing layer. Quilting is the stitching that holds these three layers together. Quilting can be done by hand or machine, in simple rows or in extravagant decorative patterns. No matter how you do it, quilted fabrics are as appealing today as they were generations ago, and the act of quilting itself is very satisfying and even relaxing.

Handquilting

Handquilting is the most traditional way to finish a quilt; it's also quite beautiful, imparting the kind of handmade goodness that can only come from a needle and thread. Handquilting requires a few specific tools, including a quilting hoop, thimble, and special needles

called *betweens*. The quilting stitch is a simple running stitch, but the following technique will help you go quickly, with a minimum of fatigue, and achieve evenly spaced stitching.

1 | Begin by sandwiching the center of the basted quilt in the hoop. Place the bottom ring of the hoop (without a screw) underneath the quilt and align the top ring of the hoop over the quilt. Slide the sections together, catching the quilt inside the hoop. Before tightening the screw, smooth the quilt sandwich in the hoop so that it is taut and check to make sure there are no tucks in the backing. Turn the screw on the outside of the hoop to set the tension.

2 | Thread a between needle with handquilting thread and knot the end. Bring the needle up from below the quilt through the top, gently tugging the knot through the backing fabric so that the knot is caught in the batting layer, and you're ready to stitch.

3 | Quilting stitches are running stitches made through all three layers of backing, batting, and quilt top. To ensure that your stitches are even on the top as well as the underside, position your nondominant hand underneath the hoop with a thimble on the middle finger.

4 | Point the needle down into the quilt top and push it through to the underside, allowing the point of the needle to tap the thimble.

5 | Once the needle taps the thimble, rock the needle forward to draw it back up and into the quilt toward the top. Continue rocking the needle through the quilt to make two or three stitches at a time. Pull the needle through, reposition the needle slightly ahead of the last stitch, and continue quilting. The idea is to make small, evenly spaced stitches.

6 | When you're close to the end of the thread, knot the thread, push the needle through the quilt top and tug the knot so that it's between the layers, and pull the needle out through the quilt top a slight distance away. Pull to secure the knot in the layers and clip the thread close to the top.

7 | Continue to quilt in sections, from the center out, repositioning the fabric in the hoop as necessary, until the quilt is completely quilted.

Machine Quilting

You can also quilt with your sewing machine, using a walking foot or a darning foot. With either foot, here are a few tips to make quilting with a machine easier:

1 | Put the machine on a table large enough to hold the entire quilt; this allows for easier maneuverability of the quilt because its weight is not pulling it. If possible,

extend the bed of the sewing machine to help distribute the weight of the quilt more evenly. Many machines offer extensions as an option, but if you don't have one, try stacking books around your machine to the bed's height as an impromptu solution.

2 | Always use a new sharp needle in the machine. There are needles specifically made for machine quilting, but I find that a fresh regular-point needle is just as good. Unlike quilting by hand, machine quilting does not require a hoop. Place your hands on top of the quilt sandwich to smooth out the area being quilted.

3 | Begin quilting in the center of the quilt top. Although it's the hardest part to manipulate under the head of the machine, beginning in the center helps prevent puckers.

4 | Manage the bulk of the quilt by tightly rolling the section that's not being quilted to fit under the arm of your sewing machine. If you like, you can purchase machine-quilting clips to hold the rolled portion and prevent it from unrolling.

5 | Adjust the height of the chair you're sitting in to machine quilt so that your vantage point is well above the bed

▶*fig. 21* |
Free-motion quilting can follow any shape.

of the machine. This prevents your shoulders from shrugging up toward your ears and causing neck and back pain.

6 | Limit your machine-quilting sessions to no more than two hours without a break. Machine quilting, especially on large quilts, can be physically arduous; it's important to take breaks.

7 | If you find it difficult to control the quilt while manipulating the quilt sandwich, consider buying quilting gloves, available at fabric stores and quilt shops. These gloves have finger and palm grips that allow you to easily maneuver the quilt top.

8 | For large quilts, consider renting time on a long-arm quilting machine (see sidebar, page 149).

Machine Quilting with a Walking Foot

Using a walking foot attachment on your sewing machine ensures that the layers of the quilt sandwich feed evenly. The walking foot does this by feeding the fabric from the top as the feed dogs pull it through from the bottom. A walking foot is ideal for quilting in straight lines or around squares and rectangles.

Free-Motion Machine Quilting with a Darning Foot

My favorite method of machine quilting uses a darning foot. You'll need to drop the feed dogs (check your owner's manual; usually this involves just turning a knob). On some machines, the feed dogs cannot be lowered, but can be covered with a feed dog cover made for the machine (check with a dealer) or a thin piece of plastic or cardboard. When you disengage or cover the feed dogs, they will no longer "drive" the fabric; you feed it by hand in any direction you choose, including from side to side. The quilting stitch can follow any shape (**fig. 21**).

This method, called free-motion quilting, is like drawing with the machine needle. The size of the stitches is determined by the speed with which you feed the quilt with your hands in combination with the speed of the needle moving up and down. This method is incredibly free-form and creative, but it takes a little getting used to. Practicing with scrap fabric and batting is essential to mastering this process, but so worth the effort.

◄ *Binding the rounded corner on Annie's Picnic Quilt (page 123) is easy with bias binding.*

BINDING + FINISHING

After quilting, the final step for a quilt or quilted project is to finish the raw edges around the perimeter. This is usually done by binding—wrapping strips of fabric around the edges and stitching. The first step is to cut strips of fabric on the straight grain or on the bias, according to the project instructions, and piece them together into one continuous strip.

Cutting and Piecing Binding Strips

Precut quilt binding strips are available for purchase at most fabric stores, but color choice is limited, and they are often crafted of either a polyester and cotton blend or poor-quality cotton. Why deprive yourself of another design opportunity? When you make your own binding strips, you can accent a fabric in the quilt top, draw attention to a design element, or introduce a new color. I prefer to use binding strips pieced with diagonal seams to avoid bulky joins. Making the binding strips is quick and easy.

1 | Begin by cutting the binding fabric into strips that are 1½" (3.8 cm) wide. Cut strips on the straight grain (lengthwise or crosswise) unless cutting on the bias is specified in the project instructions. Each project in the book lists the yardage needed for binding; cut that amount of fabric into strips.

2 | To sew the binding strips into one long length, lay two strips right sides together and perpendicular to each other. Be sure to work close to the ends of both strips.

Focusing on the square space where the strips intersect, use a fabric marker to draw a diagonal line from the top left corner of that space to the bottom right corner.

3 | Carefully pin the strips and stitch on that line **(fig. 22)**. Trim the corner as shown, leaving ¼" (6 mm) of fabric beyond the stitched line. Press the seam open.

4 | Continue adding strips until you have one continuous strip long enough to bind the entire quilt, plus at least 10" (25.5 cm) for overlapping the ends.

Attaching the Binding to the Quilt

You've now finished the quilting and removed all the safety pins. The next step is binding the quilt around the edges.

1 | Trim the layers of the quilt along the quilt top edges so they are flush. Begin attaching the binding midway along any edge of the quilt.

2 | Align the binding strip with the edge of the quilt top, right sides together, with raw edges even. Leave 10" to 12" (25.5 to 30.5 cm) of the binding free at the beginning.

Pin the binding to the quilt. Begin stitching the binding to the quilt in a ¼" (6 mm) seam **(fig. 23)**.

3 | Continue stitching along the edge, slowing down as you approach the quilt corner and stopping ¼" (6 mm) from the corner. Backstitch to secure the seam and cut the threads.

4 | To create a mitered corner, raise the presser foot and move the quilt and binding from underneath the presser foot. This allows for easy adjustments of the binding fabric. Fold back the unstitched binding at a 45° angle, bisecting the corner. This positions the binding perpendicular to the sewn section. Finger-crease the fold.

5 | Fold the unsewn binding back on itself, aligning it with the next quilt edge. The edge of the binding to be sewn should now lie flush with the quilt edge **(fig. 24)**. Starting at the corner, sew the binding along the next edge. Repeat this process on all four corners.

6 | As you're stitching along the final edge, stop stitching about 12" (30.5 cm) before the starting point. Cut the thread.

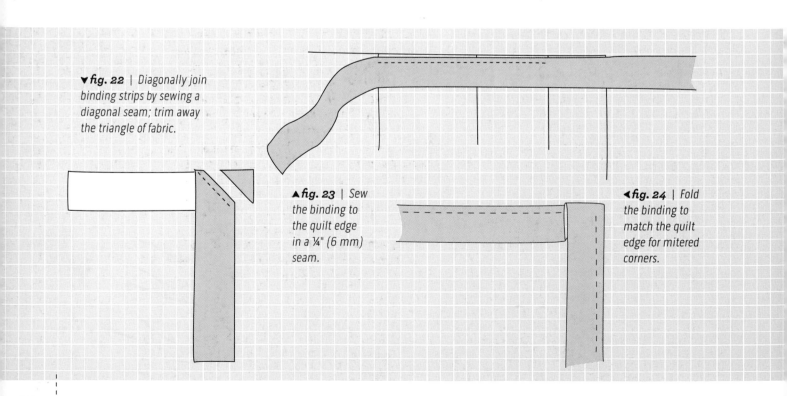

▼ **fig. 22** | *Diagonally join binding strips by sewing a diagonal seam; trim away the triangle of fabric.*

▲ **fig. 23** | *Sew the binding to the quilt edge in a ¼" (6 mm) seam.*

◄ **fig. 24** | *Fold the binding to match the quilt edge for mitered corners.*

7 | Bring the remaining binding strip and the starting tail together to meet about midway between the end and start of the binding stitches.

8 | Fold the starting tail toward the center of the quilt at a 45° angle. Finger-press the fold. Fold the ending tail away from the center of the quilt at a 45° angle. Finger-press the fold *(fig. 25)*.

9 | Unfold, and with the starting tail on top and the ending tail underneath, align the creases, right sides together, under the machine foot. Sew along the crease to create a diagonal seam. Cut the thread and trim the fabric, leaving a ¼" (6 mm) seam allowance beyond the stitching. Press the seam open.

10 | Turn the quilt over so that the quilt back is facing you. Working along the edges, pull the raw (unstitched) edge of the binding from the front of the quilt, over the quilt edges, and to the back. Pin the raw edge of the binding to the back of the quilt, folding under ¼" (6 mm) seam allowance as you pin the binding to the quilt back. The fold should lie along the stitches joining the binding to the quilt.

◄ *This small charming quilt label from philistine.com has raw side edges.*

Reproduced with permission.

11 | Handsew the binding to the backing using a slip stitch or machine sew along the edge of the binding with a zigzag stitch. A machine-sewn zigzag stitch will be visible on the front side of the binding. Your choice of thread color can minimize the contrast between the thread and binding fabric and therefore blend the two together or intentionally highlight the difference and make the zigzag stitching a graphic element.

Adding a label

A fabric label on the back of a finished quilt is a final opportunity to personalize the quilt. Consider including information about the year the quilt was made as well as who made it and whom it was made for. There is no standard size for labels—they can be any size to about 4" x 6" (10 x 15 cm). You'll often find them handstitched to the back near the lower left or right corner.

I like to embroider my labels, but you can also use fabric suitable for a printer or copy machine to print a label, combine embroidery with ink stamps, or even use fabric markers. Once you've made and decorated the label, cut it so it is ½" (1.3 cm) larger on all sides than the desired finished size. With the wrong side facing up, press a ½" (1.3 cm) seam allowance to the wrong side all around. Pin the label to the quilt back so its decorated side is visible and slip-stitch the label in place.

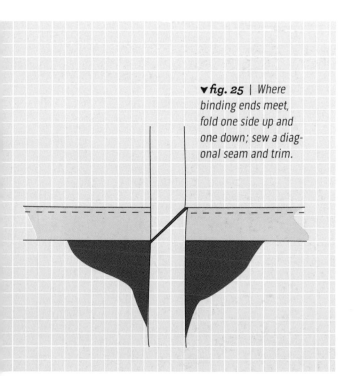

▼ *fig. 25 | Where binding ends meet, fold one side up and one down; sew a diagonal seam and trim.*

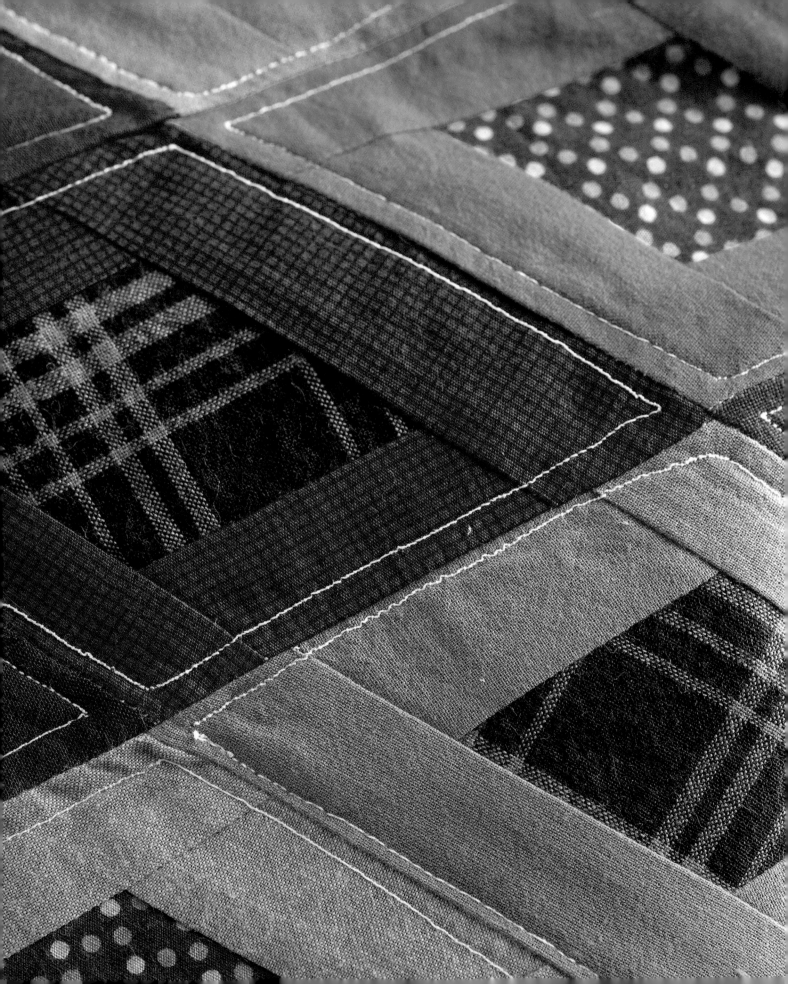

fresh patchwork projects
for home, family + friends

→ TRUE CONFESSION: Every day I wear something that I made, or carry a bag that I've sewn, or use a handcrafted potholder. And every time that a friend moves into a new house or welcomes a new baby, I craft a gift in celebration of that event. I don't do this because I'm an overachiever, but because I get so much pleasure from crafting all the little, seemingly unimportant bits of my daily life. There's something magical and empowering about choosing to make something for yourself or someone you love. You could opt to buy a potholder or a pillow or a scarf, and sometimes you will, but creating that same item out of fabric and thread transforms an otherwise mundane item. Both a handmade and a store-bought scarf will warm a neck, but the handmade one reminds you of your creativity or tells a friend how much you care. The goal of these projects is to inspire you to craft the "little things" because oftentimes they're the most cherished.

MATERIALS
These quantities will make 2 pot holders.

Assorted strips of cotton or linen in a mix of solids and prints, at least 1" (2.5 cm) wide, in varying lengths

¼ yd (23 cm) of 45" (114.5 cm) wide coordinating fabric for binding and hanging loops

⅜ yd (32 cm) of 45" (114.5 cm) wide cotton muslin

⅜ yd (32 cm) of 45" (114.5 cm) wide cotton fabric for backing

⅜ yd (32 cm) of 45" (114.5 cm) wide heat-resistant batting, such as Insul-Bright from the Warm Company

⅜ yd (32 cm) of 45" (114.5 cm) wide 100% cotton batting (do not use polyester batting because heat may melt it)

Coordinating thread for construction and quilting

TOOLS
Basic sewing tool kit (see page 15)

Quilter's clear 4" (10 cm) square ruler

FINISHED SIZE
8½" × 8½" (21.5 × 21.5 cm), 10" × 10" (25.5 × 25.5 cm), or as desired

strings attached
POT HOLDERS

I made these pot holders, along with the matching trivet on page 42, in much the same way that I cook. I added a bit of this and a pinch of that and didn't fuss too much about exact measurements. The tops for both items were pieced improvisationally using a bounty of scrap strips, or "strings." Following this recipe yields final products that burst with color and energy yet retain their usefulness, with details such as openings along the backs of the pot holders and heat-resistant batting. Whip up a batch and see if your dishes don't taste a bit better.

→ Cut the binding fabric on the crosswise grain into three 1½" (3.8 cm) wide strips.

→ From one of the binding strips, cut 2 lengths for hanging loops, each 1½" x 6" (3.8 x 15 cm).

→ Cut 2 pieces 12" x 12" (30.5 x 30.5 cm) from each of the muslin, heat-resistant batting, and cotton batting.

Making the Patchwork Pot Holder Tops

All seam allowances are ¼" (6 mm). Press seams to one side.

1 | Sew a pair of strips, right sides together, along one long edge. Press the seam and trim any excess seam allowance (see Improvisational Piecing, page 26).

2 | Pin a third strip to the already sewn pair, right sides together, along one long edge. Sew, trim, and press the seam.

3 | Repeat Steps 1 and 2 until you have 4 to 6 strips sewn together (*fig. 1*).

4 | Using a rotary cutter and self-healing cutting mat, freehand cut a 4" (10 cm) square from the joined strips, positioning the strips diagonally across the square (*fig. 2*).

5 | Repeat Steps 1 through 4 to create 4 diagonally striped blocks.

6 | Pin one pair of blocks, right sides together, so that the stripes form an inverted V at the seam. Stitch and press the seam. Trim the larger block if the blocks are not the same size. Repeat with the second pair of blocks.

7 | With right sides together, pin the sewn pairs along one long edge so that the intersection of the blocks forms a diamond shape at the center (*fig. 3*).

★TIP Use a clear quilter's 4" (10 cm) square ruler as your guide, but to maintain the improvisational quality of the blocks, don't use it for exact measurement. Rather, keep it nearby to give an approximation of size needed.

▶ *Spiral quilting lines add interest to geometric piecing.*

▲ fig. 1

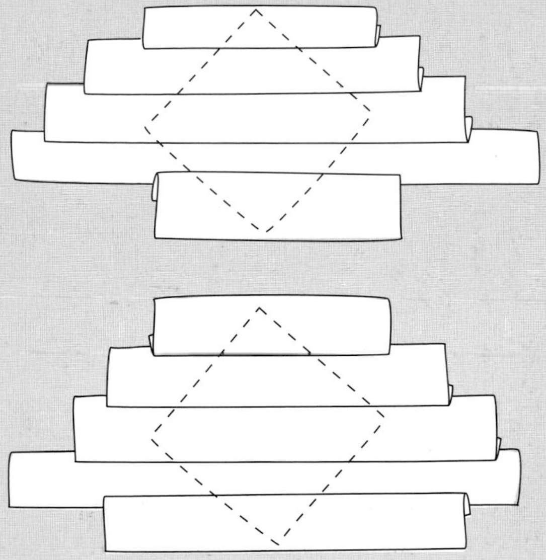

▲ fig. 2

▲ fig. 3

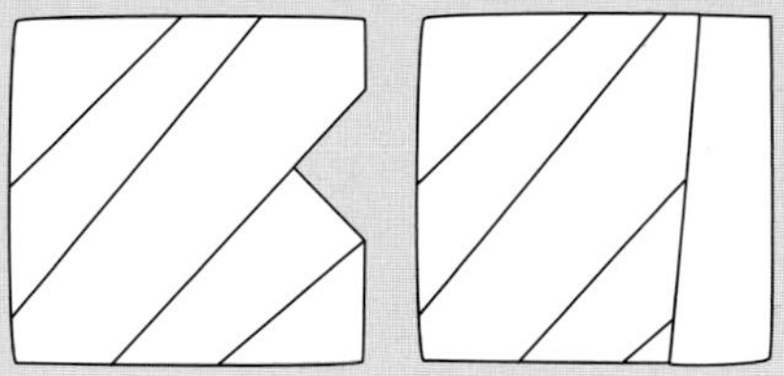

▲ fig. 4

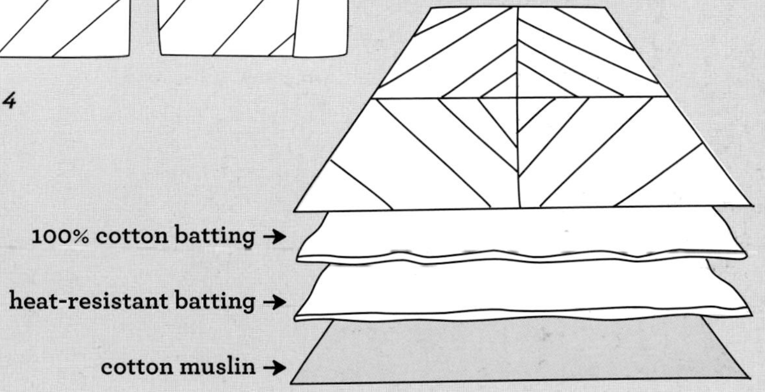

100% cotton batting →

heat-resistant batting →

cotton muslin →

▲ fig. 5

If, at any time while piecing, you discover that one of your improvisational squares is a bit small, simply add a strip along one or two sides to bring the square up to size *(fig. 4)*.

8 | Stitch, press, and trim if necessary. Repeat all steps to make a second 4-patch block for the second pot holder.

Quilting the Pot Holders

See pages 17–33 for detailed instructions on basting, quilting, trimming, and binding.

9 | On a flat surface, place a 12" × 12" (30.5 × 30.5 cm) square of cotton muslin, wrong side up. Top with a square of heat-resistant batting, then cotton batting, and finally the pot holder top, right side up *(fig. 5)*.

10 | Baste the layers together with all-purpose thread.

11 | Machine quilt the layers with coordinating thread. Mine are quilted with an improvised spiral pattern, working from the center out.

12 | Using a rotary cutter and self-healing cutting mat, trim the layers so they are flush and square.

Finishing the Pot Holders

13 | To make the envelope opening for the pot holder back, cut 1 piece of backing fabric as tall as the pot holder and 4½" (11.5 cm) wider.

14 | Using a clear quilter's ruler, rotary cutter, and self-healing cutting mat, divide the backing fabric into 2 equal pieces.

15 | Press ¼" (6 mm) to the wrong side along one long edge (the "tall" dimension). Press an additional 1¼" (3.2 cm) to the wrong side on the same edge, as shown in *fig. 6*. Edgestitch next to the inner fold and close to the outer folded edge.

16 | Repeat Step 15 with the second backing piece.

17 | On a flat surface, overlap the hemmed edges of the backing pieces 1½" (3.8 cm), with wrong sides up. Center the quilted pot holder, right side up, on top of the backing pieces; the raw edges should match (trim backing and batting as needed to match pot holder). Pin in place *(fig. 7)*.

18 | On an ironing surface, press one of the 1½" × 6" (3.8 × 15 cm) hanging loop strips in half lengthwise, wrong sides together. Open the fabric to reveal the crease running down the middle of the fabric *(fig. 8)*.

19 | Press each long edge to meet the center crease, then refold and press along the original crease, enclosing the long edges. Edgestitch both long edges and fold the strip in half to make a loop.

20 | Repeat Steps 18 and 19 to make the second pot holder loop.

Top: Zigzag stitching is a quick way to attach binding. Bottom: Split backing allows your hand to slip into the pot holder.

▲ fig. 6

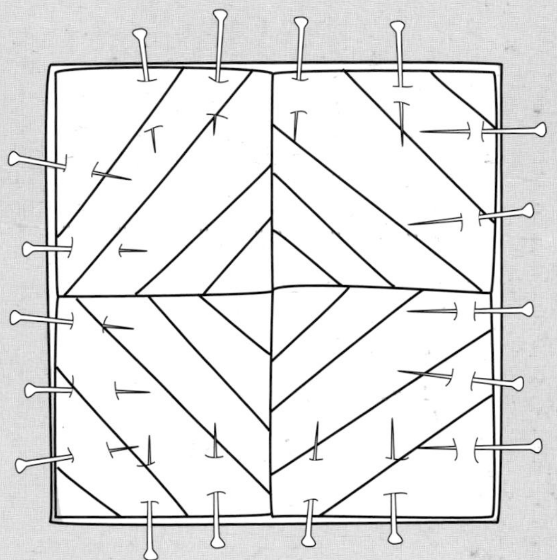

▲ fig. 7

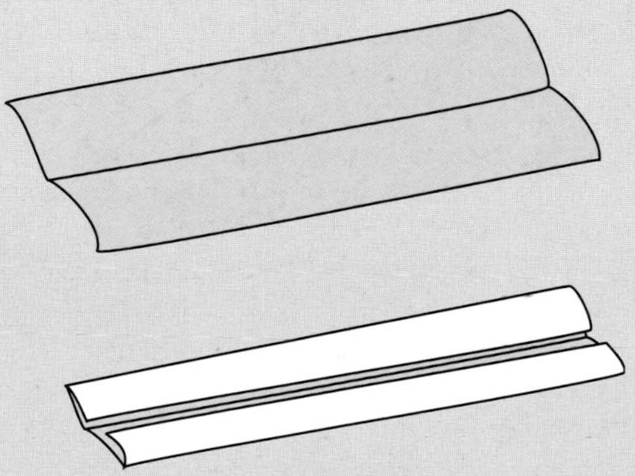

▲ fig. 8

▲ fig. 9

21 | On the backing side, baste the prepared loop into one corner with its fold toward the center and its raw edges at the pot holder raw edges (*fig. 9*).

22 | Join the binding strips using diagonal seams and stitch the binding around the pot holder front. Catch the loop ends in the seam.

23 | Fold the binding to the back, remembering to turn under the ¼" (6 mm) seam allowance, and machine or handstitch the binding to the backing. Fold the hanging loop up, over the binding, and stitch it in place so that it is visible from the front, as shown in the photograph.

MATERIALS
Assorted strips of cotton or
linen in a mix of solids and
prints, at least 1" (2.5 cm)
wide, in varying lengths

¼ yard (45.5 cm) of 45"
(114.5 cm) wide coordinating
fabric for binding

⅝ yd (57 cm) of 45" (114.5 cm)
wide cotton fabric for backing

⅝ yd (57 cm) of 45" (114.5 cm)
wide cotton muslin

⅝ yd (57 cm) of 45" (114.5 cm)
wide heat-resistant batting,
such as Insul-Bright from
The Warm Company, or 100%
cotton batting (do not use
polyester batting because
heat may melt it)

Coordinating thread for
construction and quilting

TOOLS
Basic sewing tool kit
(see page 15)

Quilter's clear 4" (10 cm)
square ruler

FINISHED SIZE
16" × 24" (40.5 × 61 cm)

strings attached
TRIVET

This trivet, designed to match the
pot holders on page 37, is sized like
a small table runner. It's made to be
practical as well as pretty, with heat-
resistant batting. Eye-catching and
fun, it'll brighten even the simplest
family meal while protecting your
table from hot dishes. Once you've
mastered the technique of strip
piecing used here, you can adapt it
for a larger quilt with ease.

- → Cut the binding fabric into three 1½" (3.8 cm) wide strips.

- → Cut one 20" x 30" (51 x 76 cm) rectangle each from the backing, muslin, and heat-resistant batting or cotton batting.

Making the Patchwork Top

All seam allowances are ¼" (6 mm). Press seams to one side.

1 | Following Steps 1 through 8 on pages 38–39, make a total of six 4-patch blocks with the strips of fabric as for the *Strings Attached Pot Holders*.

2 | Pin one pair of blocks right sides together along one edge. Stitch, press, and trim if necessary.

3 | Repeat Step 2 until you have three sewn pairs.

4 | With right sides together, pin two pairs along one long edge. Stitch, press, and trim to fit if necessary.

5 | Pin the third pair to the joined pairs, right sides together, along one long edge.

6 | Stitch, press, and trim to fit if necessary.

Quilting and Binding the Trivet

See pages 17–33 for detailed instructions on basting, quilting, trimming, and binding.

7 | On a flat surface, smooth out the backing fabric, wrong side up. Top with the heat-resistant batting, cotton batting, and then smooth the pieced trivet top, right side up, on the center of the backing and batting.

8 | Using quilter's curved safety pins, pin-baste the layers together.

9 | Using coordinating thread, hand or machine quilt the layers. Mine are quilted with improvised overlapping spirals, centered on the 4-patch units and the central joins.

10 | Using a rotary cutter, trim the layers so they are flush and square.

11 | Bind the trivet, omitting the hanging loop.

Spirals of machine quilting add vibrant movement.

Detail of trivet backing and binding. reverse side.

Strings Attached Trivet, flat view.

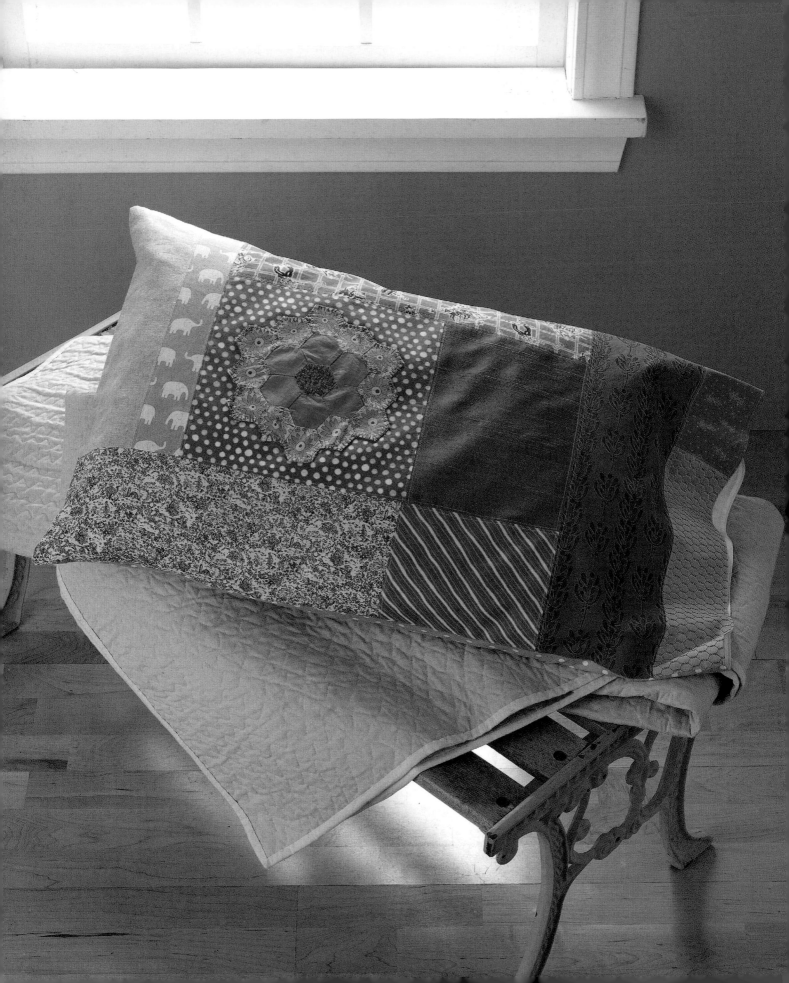

MATERIALS

Scraps or fat quarters* of 10 different cotton, linen, or silk prints and solids for sham front

¾ yd (68.5 cm) of 45" (114.5 cm) wide coordinating print or solid for sham back

Scraps or fat quarters* of 3 different prints or 3 for flower

1 yd (91.5 cm) of 45" (114.5 cm) wide white cotton muslin for sham lining

Lightweight fusible interfacing, if using silk douppioni, in amounts equal to the cut rectangles of douppioni

Coordinating thread for construction

Coordinating embroidery floss in two colors

Copy paper or freezer paper

Spray starch

*A fat quarter is an 18" × 22" (45.5 × 56 cm) cut of fabric, or ½ yd of 45" (114.5 cm) wide fabric split lengthwise. Many fabric and quilting shops offer precut fat quarters.

TOOLS

Flower Garden Sham hexagon template (page 151)

Basic sewing tool kit (page 15)

Embroidery hoop, no more than 8" (20.5 cm) diameter

Embroidery needle

FINISHED SIZE

29½" × 18½" (75 × 47 cm)

flower garden
SHAM

One of the things I love about sewing is the opportunity to play with a variety of fabrics—not just different colors and textures, but fabrics that represent different cultures and even eras. This design celebrates a diversity of textiles. It combines the traditional Grandmother's Flower Garden quilt pattern, crafted out of Depression-era fabrics using the English paper-piecing method, with contemporary Japanese prints, silk douppioni, cowboy-themed fabric, natural linen, contemporary prints, and reproduction prints. This smorgasbord works because the color palette is limited and the fabrics are cut into large, simple shapes for piecing.

→ From the 10 fat quarters, cut 1 rectangle in each of the following sizes and number the rectangles as follows:

— 1. 10" x 9¾" (25.5 x 25 cm) (shown: yellow dot)

— 2. 7" x 9¾" (18 x 25 cm) (shown: gold silk)

— 3. 16½" x 4½" (42 x 11.5 cm) (shown: cowboy print)

— 4. 2¼" x 13¾" (5.5 x 35 cm) (shown: gray elephant print)

— 5. 4¼" x 13¾" (11 x 35 cm) (shown: natural linen)

— 6. 15½" x 5¾" (39.5 x 14.5 cm) (shown: toile print)

— 7. 7" x 5¾" (18 x 14.5 cm) (shown: yellow stripe)

— 8. 5½" x 19" (14 x 48.5 cm) (shown: mustard and gray print)

— 9. 3½" x 13¼" (9 x 33.5 cm) (shown: light yellow print)

— 10. 3½" x 6¼" (9 x 16 cm) (shown: light yellow-green print)

→ From backing fabric, cut 1 piece measuring 30" x 19" (76 x 48.5 cm).

→ From cotton muslin, cut 2 pieces measuring 30" x 19" (76 cm x 48.5 cm).

Detail of flower appliqué made from pieced hexagons.

Making the Hexagon Flower

All seam allowances are ¼" (6 mm) unless otherwise indicated.

1 | Trace or copy the hexagon template on page 151 onto copy paper or freezer paper and cut out; you will need a total of 19 paper hexagons. Refer to page 26 for details on English paper piecing.

2 | Apply spray starch to the scrap intended for the flower center and press.

3 | Lay the starched and pressed fabric, wrong side up, on a self-healing cutting mat. Pin a paper hexagon to the fabric.

4 | Lay the clear acrylic ruler or square along one edge of the pinned hexagon so that the ruler extends ¼" (6 mm) beyond the template edge. Using a rotary cutter, cut along the ruler's edge for the length of one hexagon side. You are adding a ¼" (6 mm) seam allowance to the paper template.

5 | Reposition the ruler along a second edge, remembering to place the ruler's edge ¼" (6 mm) beyond the paper hexagon's edge. Cut along this edge *(fig. 1)*. Continue repositioning and cutting all six hexagon sides.

6 | Press the ¼" (6 mm) seam allowance to the wrong side, over the paper template; do not remove the paper piece *(fig. 2)*.

7 | With a handsewing needle and thread, catch the seam allowances at the hexagon corners with small stitches, being careful not to sew into the paper template, as shown in the illustrations for English paper piecing, page 26.

8 | Repeat Steps 2 through 7 to make 18 more hexagons from the remaining 2 scraps of fabric for the flower. The flower has three tiers of hexagons, each cut from a different fabric: the first tier is 1 center hexagon; the second tier consists of 6 hexagons, shown in purple fabric; and the outer tier consists of 12 hexagons, shown in patterned fabric.

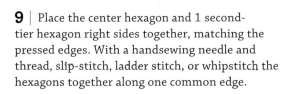

▲ fig. 1

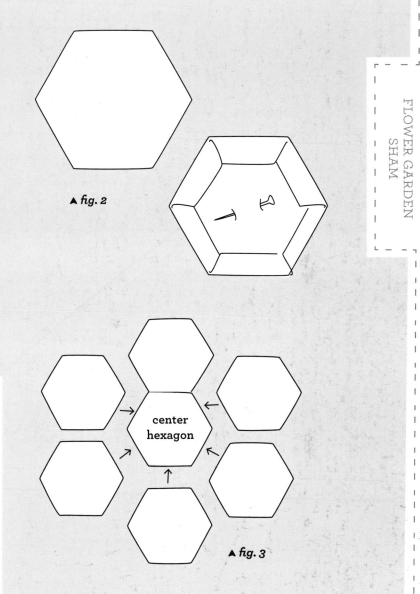

▲ fig. 2

▲ fig. 3

center hexagon

9 | Place the center hexagon and 1 second-tier hexagon right sides together, matching the pressed edges. With a handsewing needle and thread, slip-stitch, ladder stitch, or whipstitch the hexagons together along one common edge.

10 | Open out the joined hexagons. Position a third hexagon so that it can be sewn to one edge of each previous hexagon, as shown in **fig. 3**. Continue to attach second-tier hexagons, one at a time, until all 6 have been sewn to the center hexagon.

11 | Stitch the third-tier hexagons, one at a time, to the previously joined hexagons. The outside seam allowances of the third-tier hexagons are not joined to other patches but remain pressed down.

12 | Carefully remove the paper templates from the flower and press. Center and pin the hexagon flower to Rectangle 1 and secure the rectangle in an embroidery hoop.

13 | Embroider French knots (see page 24) densely in the center hexagon, using 6 strands of embroidery floss in two coordinating colors.

14 | Thread the embroidery needle with 3 strands of floss. Using blanket stitch (see page 23), simultaneously embroider and appliqué the hexagon flower to the background fabric, repositioning the fabric in the hoop if necessary.

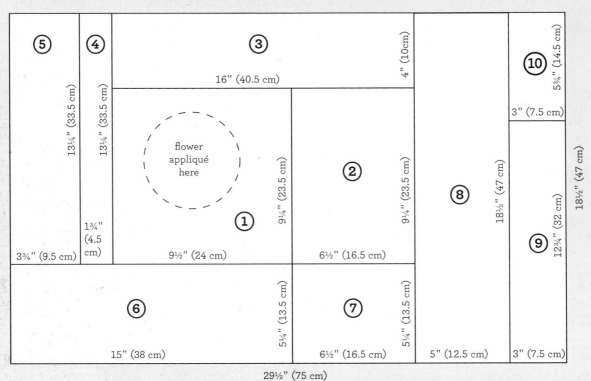

▲ *fig. 4 (showing finished measurements)*

The figure shows a rectangular layout with numbered sections:

- ⑤ 13¼" (33.5 cm) tall
- ④ 13¼" (33.5 cm) tall
- ③ 16" (40.5 cm) wide
- ⑩ 5¾" (14.5 cm); 3" (7.5 cm)
- flower appliqué here
- ① 9½" (24 cm); 1¾" (4.5 cm)
- 3¾" (9.5 cm)
- ② 9¼" (23.5 cm); 6½" (16.5 cm)
- 9¼" (23.5 cm)
- 4" (10cm)
- ⑧ 18½" (47 cm)
- ⑨ 12¾" (32 cm)
- ⑥ 15" (38 cm); 5¼" (13.5 cm)
- ⑦ 6½" (16.5 cm); 5¼" (13.5 cm)
- 5" (12.5 cm)
- 3" (7.5 cm)
- 18½" (47 cm)
- 29½" (75 cm)

Sewing Front of Sham

Unless otherwise noted, press seams open. If using silk douppioni, fuse interfacing to the fabric wrong side before sewing, following the manufacturer's instructions.

15 | Referring to *fig. 4*, pin Rectangle 1, with its appliquéd hexagon flower, to Rectangle 2, right sides together, along one 9¾"(25 cm) edge.

16 | Sew together by machine. Press the seam open. Topstitch ⅛" (3 mm) from the seam on both sides.

17 | Referring to *fig. 4*, continue pinning, sewing, pressing, and topstitching Rectangles 3, 4, and 5 in order.

The pillow back is made from polka-dot fabric.

18 | Pin Rectangles 6 and 7, right sides together, along one short edge. Sew and press the seam open. Topstitch ⅛" (3 mm) from the seam on both sides.

19 | Pin the joined pair to the pieced unit, right sides together, along their long edges, referring to the construction diagram for placement. Sew, press, and topstitch as before.

20 | Referring to the construction diagram, pin and sew Rectangle 8 to the pieced unit. Press the seam open and topstitch as before.

21 | Join Rectangles 9 and 10 along one short edge. Sew, press, and topstitch as before.

22 | Referring to the construction diagram, pin the sewn pair to the main section, right sides together, along the indicated edge. Sew, press, and topstitch.

Finishing the Sham

23 | Pin the pieced sham front to the backing fabric, right sides together. Using a ¼" (6 mm) seam allowance, sew the two long sides and the edge along Rectangle 5 together. Trim the corners to reduce bulk, being careful not to cut through the stitching. Turn the sham right side out and press flat. Set aside.

24 | Pin the 2 muslin lining pieces with right sides together. Using a ¼" (6 mm) seam allowance, sew two long sides and one short side together. Trim the corners, being careful not to cut through the stitching. Press flat.

25 | Press ¼" (6 mm) to the wrong side along the open edges of both the pillow sham and the lining. Slip the lining into the assembled sham with wrong sides together. Pin the pressed edges of the sham and lining together, matching the folded edges and seams.

26 | Topstitch the edges together ⅛" (3 mm) from the pressed edges.

 ## machine-quilting tips

There is definitely a learning curve for machine quilting. Here are a few tips that can make that curve a little less steep.

→ **ALWAYS** start quilting in the middle of the quilt top to avoid puckering.

→ **MANAGE** the bulk of the quilt by tightly rolling the section that you're not working on so that it will fit under the arm of the machine. Specially designed clips are available at fabric and quilting stores that help prevent your quilt from unrolling.

→ **ADJUST** the height of your chair so that your vantage point is well above the bed of the machine. This prevents your shoulders from shrugging up toward your ears and causing neck and back pain.

→ **LIMIT** your machine-quilting sessions to no more than two hours without a break. Machine quilting can be physically arduous, especially when working on large quilts, and it's important to take breaks.

→ **IF** you have difficulty manipulating the quilt sandwich, try wearing a pair of quilting gloves, available at fabric and quilting stores. These gloves have finger and palm grips and allow you to easily maneuver the quilt top.

MATERIALS
8 to 12 strips of scrap fabric, each at least 1" × 6" (2.5 × 15 cm).

NOTE *The width can vary along a single strip for Version A, with 1" (2.5 cm) as the minimum width. For Version B, the minimum strip width is 1½" (3.8 cm). See the instructions for details.*

2 pieces of cotton muslin, each measuring 8" × 8" (20.5 × 20.5 cm)

2 pieces of coordinating lining fabric, each measuring 5¾" × 5" (14.5 × 12.5 cm)

Scrap fabric measuring 1½" × 3" (3.8 × 7.5 cm) for loop (optional)

Coordinating thread for construction and quilting

7" (18 cm) polyester zipper

TOOLS
Basic sewing tool kit (see page 15)

Tracing paper

FINISHED SIZE
5¼" × 4½" (13.5 × 11.5 cm)

scrap-busting
COIN PURSE

When is a scrap too small to keep? If you consider the size of the scraps that make up this small but incredibly useful coin purse, the answer is almost never. It's a quick and easy project and a wonderful way to preserve a few precious fragments of a much-loved fabric. These are such fun to piece that I sewed up two sample versions, one that's improvisationally pieced in a variety of bright colors and a second that features a more limited palette of fabrics.

Making the Patchwork

All seam allowances are ¼" (6 mm). Press seams to one side, alternating sides where seams meet.

1 | Version A features a brown print fabric alternated with various colored strips. Version B is made from yellow and green prints alternated with gray solid fabric.

Version A

2 | From tracing paper, measure and cut a rectangle 5¾" × 5" (14.5 × 12.5 cm) for purse pattern.

3 | Pin 2 strips, right sides together, and sew one long edge. Press.

4 | Pin a third strip to the sewn pair, right sides together, and sew one long edge. Press.

5 | Continue pinning, sewing, and pressing strips, alternating brown strips with colored strips, until the sewn piece measures about 6" × 8" (15 × 20 cm). The seams between strips do not need to be parallel; using strips with varying widths makes the patchwork more interesting.

6 | Using a rotary cutter and ruler, cut the block of sewn strips roughly perpendicular to the seams to create two unequal sections *(fig. 1)*.

7 | Repeat Steps 2 through 5 to make a second pair of sewn strips.

8 | Pin a primarily brown strip to one section from Step 6, right sides together, with the new strip perpendicular to the sewn strips. Sew and press the seam *(fig. 2)*.

9 | Pin another section of sewn strips to the remaining long raw edge of the new strip from Step 8, right sides together, and sew. For greatest variety, choose the second pieced section from the other pair constructed in Step 7; slip it up or down in relation to the first pieced section (the top and bottom don't need to be even), or trim the uneven edge of the pieced section and

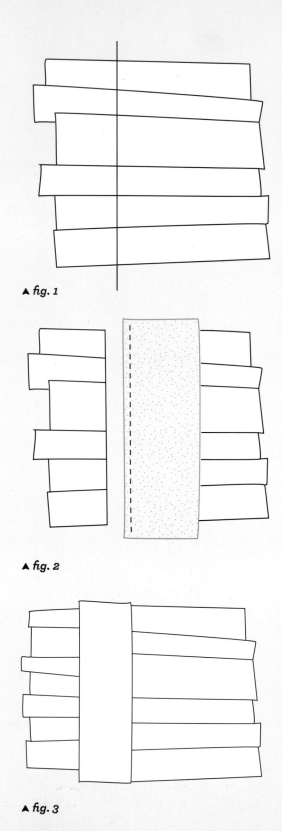

▲ *fig. 1*

▲ *fig. 2*

▲ *fig. 3*

rotate it 180° before attaching it to the other side of the new strip *(fig. 3)*. Make sure the final arrangement yields a pieced area large enough to cut 1 pattern piece.

10 | Pin the paper pattern to the patchwork block, right sides up. Trim the sewn piece to the pattern size.

11 | Repeat Steps 8 through 10 to make the second coin purse side.

Version B

12 | From tracing paper, measure and cut a rectangle 5¾" × 5" (14.5 × 12.5 cm) for the purse pattern.

13 | For this version, cut the strips either 1½" (3.8 cm) or 2" (5 cm) wide and 6" (15 cm) long. Cut several of each width from the gray solid (A) and from the green and yellow scraps (B).

14 | Join strips side by side, alternating 1½" (3.8 cm) A strips and 2" (5 cm) B strips to create patchwork fabric at least 7" × 6" (18 × 15 cm). Join alternating 2" (5 cm) A strips and 1½" (3.8 cm) B strips to make a second patchwork block at least 7" × 6" (18 × 15 cm).

15 | Use a rotary cutter to cut one of the patchwork blocks into two unequal sections, cutting perpendicular to the seams between strips. Sew

▲ *Narrowly spaced lines of quilting are quick and easy on this project.*

one of the sections to each side of the second patch-work block, matching the seamlines *(fig. 4)*.

16 | Using the pattern piece, cut two coin purse sides from the pieced fabric. Position the pattern so a vertical seam between pieced blocks is slightly off center on each piece.

Sewing the Coin Purse

17 | Layer 1 muslin square, wrong side up, and one coin purse side, right side up, on a flat surface. Pin the layers together.

18 | Machine quilt the layers as desired, removing pins as you work. Trim the muslin to match the coin purse fabric.

19 | Repeat Steps 17 and 18 with the second coin purse side.

20 | By hand or machine, make several stitches very close together across the closed zipper teeth, 5¾" (14.5 cm) from the top end of the zipper tape. To work by machine, set the machine for its widest zigzag stitch and a length of 0.1 mm. Turn the hand wheel through one full rotation to ensure the needle will clear the zipper teeth before sewing. These stitches will act as a new zipper stop. With scissors, trim the excess zipper just beyond the stitched zipper stop.

21 | Press ¼" (6 mm) to the wrong side along one long edge of each piece of lining fabric.

22 | With a fabric marking pen, mark a dot along the folded edge of each lining piece, ½" (1.3 cm) from each side edge. With right side up, pin the folded edge of 1 lining piece to the wrong side of the zipper tape, with the fold ⅛" (3 mm) from the zipper teeth *(fig. 5)*.

23 | With a zipper foot, edgestitch the lining to the zipper tape between the two dots, backstitching at each end of the seam.

24 | Repeat Steps 22 and 23 to attach the second side of the lining to the other zipper tape.

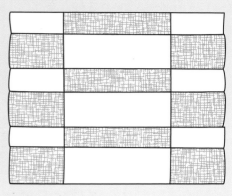

▲ *fig. 4*

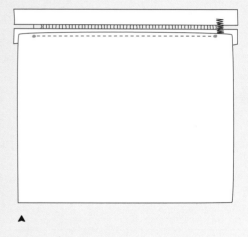

▲

25 | Press ¼" (6 mm) to the wrong side along one long edge of 1 purse piece. Mark a dot ½" (1.3 cm) from each end on the purse fabric right side, along the folded edge.

26 | With right sides facing up, pin the prepared purse fabric to the zipper tape, ⅛" (3 mm) from the zipper teeth.

27 | Starting at the marked dot and using a zipper foot, edgestitch the purse fabric to the zipper tape between the two dots, backstitching at each end of the seam.

28 | Repeat Steps 25 through 27 with the second purse fabric piece. *Important: partially open the zipper*

before continuing. Pin the lining pieces right sides together, making sure not to catch the purse fabric in the seam.

29 | Sew the lining fabric pieces together along the sides and bottom, leaving a 4" (10 cm) gap along the bottom edge.

30 | For optional loop: Fold the 1½" × 3" (3.8 × 7.5 cm) scrap in half, wrong sides together, and press. Open the fold and press the two long edges to meet at the center fold. Press again. Refold the strip along the original crease and press once more, enclosing the raw edges. Topstitch ⅛" (3 mm) from both long edges. Fold the strip in half to form a loop, matching the raw edges. Pin the loop to one side of the purse,

1" (2.5 cm) below the zipper, with the fold toward the purse center and the raw edges matched. Stitch ⅛" (3 mm) from the raw edges.

31 | Pin the purse pieces right sides together. Sew the purse sides and bottom, catching the loop in the seam. Trim the lower corners of the purse and lining to reduce bulk. Turn the purse right side out.

32 | Ease the purse corners into place with a point turner, pencil eraser, or other blunt object, and press the purse flat. Press the seam allowance along the gap in the lining seam to the wrong side and machine stitch the gap closed. Tuck the lining into the purse.

▲ *Put aside small scraps of fabric to use for these quick coin purses.*

MATERIALS

For each coaster:

12 to 20 scrap strips of various cotton prints and solids, each 1" to 2" (2.5 to 5 cm) wide and 4" to 6" (10 to 15 cm) long

Fat quarter (18" × 22" [45.5 × 56 cm]) of coordinating fabric for binding

7" × 7" (18 × 18 cm) scrap of coordinating cotton fabric for backing

7" × 7" (18 × 18 cm) scrap of cotton batting

Coordinating thread for construction and quilting

TOOLS

Basic sewing tool kit (see page 15)

Purchased circle template, or tracing paper and cup or bowl of desired size to create a template

FINISHED SIZE

5¾" (14.5 cm) in diameter

round + round
COASTERS

If our glasses have round bases, why do I always make square coasters? This was my daughter's innocent question. "I don't," I said—and then I set about designing these. Coasters are perfect projects for using scraps and trying new techniques. This design encourages you to piece strips improvisationally, combine a variety of fabrics, and maybe even try your hand at free-motion machine quilting.

→ Using a rotary cutter, quilter's clear acrylic ruler, and cutting mat, cut the binding fabric into enough 1½" (3.8 cm) bias strips to equal at least 20" (51 cm).

Making the Patchwork

All seam allowances are ¼" (6 mm). Press seams to one side.

1 | Pin 2 of your fabric scrap strips, right sides together, along one long edge. Stitch the seam and press to one side.

2 | Pin a third strip to the sewn pair, right sides together, along one long edge. Stitch the seam and press to one side.

3 | Continue sewing together groups of 3 to 5 strips to make a total of 4 pieced strip sections, each at least 3½" (9 cm) square *(fig. 1)*.

4 | Pin 2 pieced strip sections, right sides together, so that their strips lie perpendicular to each other. Using the straight edge of one strip as a guide, sew the 2 squares together. Trim the uneven edges along the seam *(fig. 2)*, leaving a ¼" (6 mm) seam allowance, and press the seam toward the long strip to reduce bulk *(fig. 3)*.

5 | Repeat Step 4 with the remaining pieced units. Press the seam toward the long strip.

6 | Pin the assembled units, right sides together, matching the center seams, with the strips again running perpendicular across the next seamline. The pressed seam allowances will lie in opposite directions, nesting together at the center point for minimum bulk. Stitch the seam and press it to one side. You now have a single unit of stitched fabric strips.

7 | Place the pieced unit on your cutting mat. Create a circle template, if none is available, by tracing or drawing a 5¾" (14.5 cm) circle onto tracing paper.

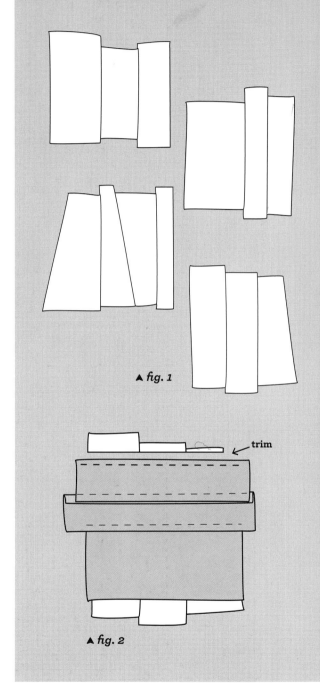

▲ *fig. 1*

trim

▲ *fig. 2*

Place the circle template on the fabric and secure it with pins or weights or trace around the template with a fabric marker. In keeping with the coaster's improvisational design, position the intersecting seamlines slightly off-center. With a rotary cutter or scissors, cut the circle shape from the pieced fabric *(fig. 4)*.

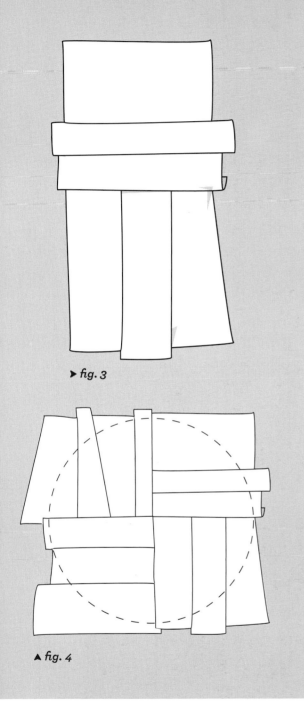

▶ fig. 3

▲ fig. 4

▲ *Bias binding goes smoothly around the curved shape.*

Quilting and Binding the Coaster

See pages 17–33 for detailed instructions on basting, quilting, trimming, and binding.

8 | Place the backing fabric, wrong side up, on the cutting mat. Layer the batting and coaster top, right side up, over the backing fabric. Secure the three layers with 1 or 2 curved safety pins.

9 | Using the rotary cutter on the mat, trim the batting and backing to match the coaster top.

10 | Drop the feed dogs on your sewing machine and free-motion machine quilt the coaster, starting at the central seamline intersection and spiraling out to the edges. Remove safety pins as you work.

11 | Sew binding strips together using diagonal seams, if necessary, to create a strip at least 20" (51 cm) long.

12 | Sew binding to coaster, overlapping the ends, as you would bind a quilt. The bias strips will curve easily around the round shape of the coaster. Turn under ¼" (6 mm) on the binding's unstitched edge and pin the binding to the coaster wrong side. Hand or machine stitch binding to backing.

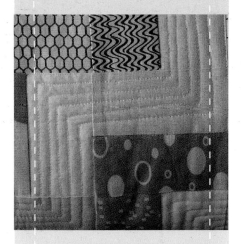

MATERIALS

Cotton and linen print scraps in an assortment of mostly white colorways, each measuring at least 4" × 2¼" (10 × 5.5 cm), for a total of about ½ yd (45.5 cm)

Cotton and linen scraps in solid whites and creams, each measuring at least 4" × 2¼" (10 × 5.5 cm), for a total of about ½ yd (45.5 cm)

¾ yd (68.5 cm) of 45" (114.5 cm) wide cotton fabric for backing

¾ yd (68.5 cm) of cotton batting

1½ yd (137 cm) of 45" (114.5 cm) wide cotton muslin to make pillow form

3 yd (2.8 m) packaged piping OR ½ yd (45.5 cm) coordinating cotton fabric and 3 yd (2.8 m) of ⁶⁄₃₂" (5 mm) cord

12 oz (340 g) polyester fiberfill

Coordinating thread for construction and quilting

16" (40.5 cm) polyester zipper

TOOLS

Basic sewing tool kit (see page 15)

FINISHED SIZE

14" × 31½" (35.5 × 80 cm)

zigzag
PILLOW

The top of this appealing pillow is a simple repeated block. For a fresh, contemporary look, my fabrics are primarily white with simple graphic patterns, paired with creams and whites to subtly hint at the zigzag design. The pillow's shape, accented by piping around the edge, is perfect for use on a bed, sofa, or loveseat, and its unusual size allows you to make your own pillow form and decide how full you'd like the pillow to be.

→ From the assorted prints, cut 36 rectangles measuring 4" x 2¼" (10 x 5.5 cm).

→ From the assorted solids, cut 36 rectangles measuring 4" x 2¼" (10 x 5.5 cm).

→ From backing fabric, cut 2 pieces measuring 18" x 22" (45.5 x 56 cm).

→ From 1 yd (91.5 cm) of muslin, cut 2 pieces measuring 14½" x 32" (37 x 81.5 cm). Reserve the remaining ½ yd (45.5 cm) of muslin.

→ From piping fabric, cut 1½" (3.8 cm) wide strips on the bias, totaling at least 110" (2.8 m), if not using packaged piping

Making the Patchwork

All seam allowances are ¼" (6 mm). Press all seams to one side, alternating sides where seams intersect.

1 | Pin 1 print rectangle and 1 solid rectangle, right sides together, along one long edge. Sew and press the seam. Repeat to make a total of thirty-six 2-patch blocks *(fig. 1)*.

2 | Pin a pair of blocks, right sides together, so that the rectangles in one block are perpendicular to the rectangles in the second block. Sew and press. Repeat to create a total of eight 4-patch blocks with solid rectangles adjacent (A block), and eight 4-patch blocks with print rectangles adjacent (B block) *(fig. 2)*. Reserve the remaining 4 blocks.

3 | Following the construction diagram, pin an A block to a B block, right sides together, along one long edge *(fig. 3)*. Sew and press. Repeat to create a total of eight 8-patch blocks.

4 | Pin two 8-patch blocks together. Sew and press seam. Repeat to make a total of four sections with 16 patches in each. Notice the relative positions of the print and solid patches to create a zigzag pattern *(fig. 4)*.

5 | Lay the four assembled sections on a flat surface and check the integrity of the zigzag pattern. Pin, sew, and press the four rectangular sections together.

6 | Arrange the last 4 blocks along the right edge of the assembled pillow top, maintaining the orientation necessary for the zigzag pattern *(fig. 5)*. Join the blocks into a 4-block strip. Sew the strip to the assembled pillow top to complete it.

Basting and Quilting the Pillow Top

See pages 17–33 for detailed instructions on basting and quilting the patchwork pillow top.

7 | Place the reserved ½ yd (45.5 cm) of muslin, wrong side up, on a flat surface. Layer the cotton batting and the pillow top, right side up, on the muslin. Pin-baste the layers together with quilter's curved safety pins.

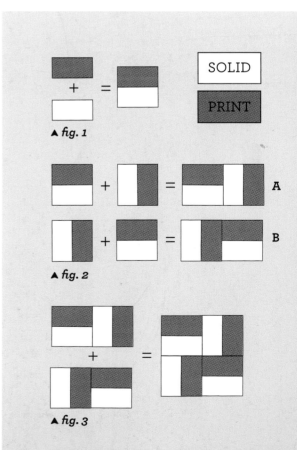

▲ *fig. 1*

SOLID

PRINT

▲ *fig. 2*

A

B

▲ *fig. 3*

8 | Hand or machine quilt as desired, removing pins as you quilt. I machine quilted lines spaced ¼" (6 mm) apart on the solid fabrics only to highlight the zigzag arrangement of the graphic prints.

Making and Attaching Piping

Note: If using purchased piping, skip to Step 13. To make your own piping, attach a zipper foot to the sewing machine.

9 | Using diagonal seams, join the 1½" (3.8 cm) strips of piping fabric to create a continuous strip at least 110" (2.8 m) long.

10 | Fold the strip's long edges, wrong sides together, so the raw edges meet. Lay the cord in the center of the fabric strip, aligning one end of the cord with the strip end, so the cord lies inside the folded fabric. Pin the cord and folded fabric at the end.

Whites and creams form a subtle zigzag pattern.

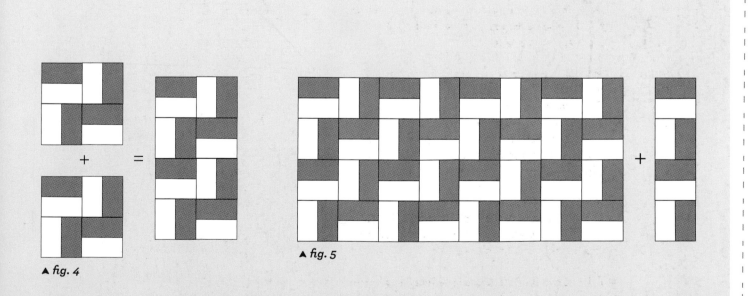

▲ fig. 4

▲ fig. 5

11 | Using a zipper foot, stitch close to the cord, about ¼" (6 mm) away from the folded edge, along the entire length of the fabric strip, encasing the cord as you work.

12 | Trim the piping seam allowance a scant ¼" (5 mm) from the stitches.

13 | Beginning near the center of one long edge, pin the piping to the pillow top, right sides together, aligning the piping raw edge with the pillow top raw edge. The line of stitches on the piping will lie just outside the pillow top's ¼" (6 mm) seamline. Using the zipper foot, sew the piping to the pillow top along the first row of stitches, leaving the first 3" (7.5 cm) of piping free and stopping ¼" (6 mm) from the corner. Backstitch, then lift the foot and pull the fabric away from the foot. Cut the threads.

14 | Clip into the piping seam allowance where the piping meets the pillow top's corner, clipping almost to, but not through, the stitching. Fold the cord around the corner, allowing the clipped seam allowance to open up. Pivot the fabric to sew along the second side, lower the presser foot, and continue around the top, turning the corners as before, stopping about 3" (7.5 cm) before the starting point.

*TIP If your needle position is adjustable, move the needle slightly to the left (0.5 to 1 mm), away from the cord. By placing these stitches slightly farther away, you lessen the possibility that they will be visible in the finished pillow. Turn the hand wheel through one complete stitch to make sure the needle won't strike the foot.

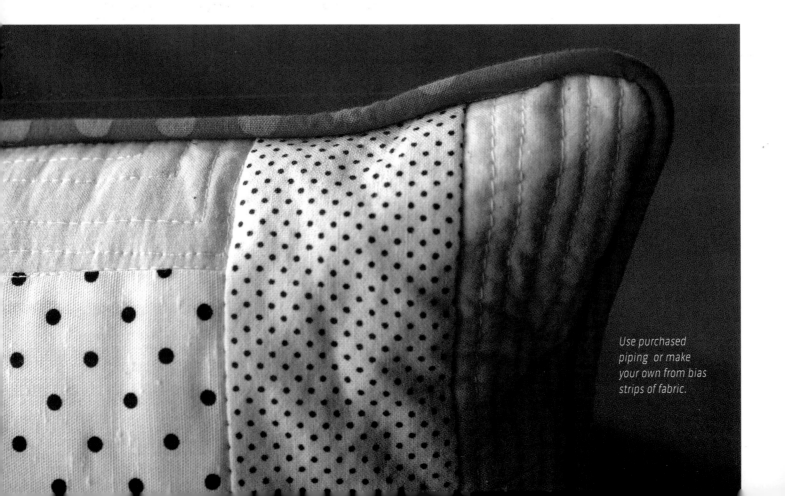

Use purchased piping or make your own from bias strips of fabric.

15 | Trim the cord end so that it overlaps the beginning by 1" (2.5 cm). Using a seam ripper, undo 1" (2.5 cm) of stitching at the piping end and expose the cording there.

16 | Trim 1" (2.5 cm) from the end of the exposed cording so it meets the cord from the beginning of the piping without overlapping. Do not cut the fabric covering the cording; if necessary, pull the cording slightly to expose more than 1" (2.5 cm), returning the cording to its original position after cutting. Smooth the fabric back into place; 1" (2.5 cm) of piping fabric will be without cording.

17 | Fold ½" (1.3 mm) of piping fabric to the wrong side at the empty end and finger-press. Slip the beginning of the piping (with its cording) into the pressed end of the piping. The cording ends will abut, and the pressed edge will overlap the piping raw edge by ½" (1.3 cm).

18 | Reposition the piping and pillow top under the zipper foot and finish attaching the piping to the pillow top.

Finishing the Pillow

19 | Referring to the sidebar on page 106 for inserting a zipper in a pillow back, attach the zipper to the backing fabric pieces along one short edge.

20 | Working on a table covered with a self-healing mat, layer the zippered backing, right side up, and the pillow top, wrong side up, with the zipper centered on the pillow top. Pin the pillow top and backing. Trim the backing so it is flush with the pillow top edges, being careful not to cut off the zipper pull.

21 | Slide the zipper pull to a point midway between the pillow edges before stitching around the pillow perimeter. Using a zipper foot, sew the backing to the pillow top along all four sides. TIP: Sew with the pillow on top and position the stitches just inside the previous rows of piping stitches, closer to the cording. Adjust the needle position, if possible. The zipper foot will still ride along the edge of the cording, but the stitches will

be slightly closer to the cording. Clip the corners to reduce bulk, being careful not to cut through the stitching.

22 | Turn the pillow top right side out through the zipper opening.

23 | Use a point turner or other tool to gently smooth the corners into position. Tugging gently on the piping will help. Press the pillow flat.

Making the Pillow Form

24 | Pin the muslin pieces around their edges, right sides together.

25 | Sew the pieces together, leaving a 10" (25.5 cm) opening for turning along one long side. Clip the corners. Turn right side out and press, pressing the seam allowances along the opening to the wrong side as you go.

26 | Stuff with polyester fiberfill until the desired firmness is reached.

27 | Tucking in the seam allowances along the opening, handsew the opening closed with a slip stitch.

▲ *A lapped zipper insertion makes a neat finish for a pillow back.*

MATERIALS
6 to 8 cotton, linen, and silk scraps in solid red and red-and-white prints, each measuring at least 4" × 7" (10 × 18 cm)

¼ yard (23 cm) of 45" (114.5 cm) wide red cotton corduroy for backing

Coordinating thread for construction and topstitching

One 1⅛" (28 mm) button

TOOLS
Basic sewing tool kit (see page 15)

Pattern paper (or substitute butcher paper, craft paper, or unprinted newsprint)

FINISHED SIZE
3¾" × 25½" (9.5 × 65 cm)

peppermint
NECK WARMER

As an avid knitter, I've made several neck warmers in wool, but this fabric version suits my Texas climate. For those lucky enough to see snow every year, this fun neck cozy can team up with a traditional neck warmer and provide just a wee bit more warmth. I used six different fabric scraps for the peppermint mix—a solid red silk douppioni and five different red-and-white cotton prints.

➜ From fabric scraps, freehand-cut 25 to 30 strips on the bias, each from 1½" to 2¼" (3.8 to 5.5 cm) wide and about 5" (12.5 cm) long

➜ From corduroy backing fabric, cut a piece on the bias measuring 4¼" x 26" (11 x 66 cm). Piece as necessary.

➜ From a leftover scrap of one of the red-and-white cotton prints, cut 1 piece measuring 1½" x 2 ½" (3.8 cm x 6.5 cm) for button loop.

Making the Patchwork

All seam allowances are ¼" (6 mm). Press seams to one side.

1 | Draw a 4¼" × 26" (11 × 66 cm) rectangle on pattern paper and cut out. Set aside.

2 | Pin 2 scrap strips, right sides together, along the long edges. Sew and press the seam to one side. Remember that the bias strips will stretch easily and be careful not to distort them as you sew. Do not trim the strip ends even but work toward creating a long, narrow rectangle as you piece.

3 | Pin a second strip to the sewn pair, right sides together, along one long edge. Sew and press.

4 | Continue pinning and sewing strips to the sewn unit until the piece measures at least 28" (71 cm); this is the neck warmer front. It's okay if the short ends are not perpendicular to the long edges.

5 | Place the neck warmer front strip on a self-healing cutting mat, right side up. Position the paper pattern on top of the long pieced strip, angling it slightly across the strips, so the pattern's long edges are not quite perpendicular to the strips. Secure the pattern piece with pins or pattern weights.

6 | Using a rotary cutter, carefully cut around the perimeter of the pattern. Remove the pins and set aside.

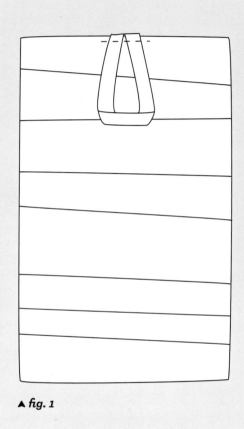

▲ **fig. 1**

7 | To make the button loop, fold the strip in half, lengthwise, with wrong sides together. Press to form a crease.

8 | Open the strip and fold the long edges inward to meet at the center crease. Press. Refold along the center crease and press again, enclosing the raw edges. Topstitch ⅛" (3 mm) from both long edges.

9 | With a removable fabric marker, mark the mid-point of one short edge on the neck warmer front strip. Fold the button loop in half and pin it to the right side of the neck warmer at the mark, aligning the raw edges, with the loop fold toward the center of the neck warmer. Machine baste in place ⅛" (3 mm) from the raw edges *(fig. 1)*.

Sewing the Neck Warmer

10 | Pin the neck warmer front strip to the corduroy backing strip, right sides together. Sew together, leaving an 8" (20.5 cm) opening near the center of one long edge for turning.

11 | Clip the corners and turn the neck warmer right side out. Push corners out gently with a point turner, pencil eraser, or other blunt object, and pull out the button loop. Press the neck warmer flat, pressing from the front to avoid flattening the corduroy pile. Use a press cloth to cover the piecing, especially if it includes silk or delicate fabrics. As you press, turn the seam allowances along the opening to the wrong side and press.

12 | Pin the front and backing together along the opening. Topstitch ⅛" (3 mm) from all edges of the neck warmer, removing pins as you reach them.

13 | Try on the neck warmer and mark the button placement as desired; sew the button in place.

▲ *Use a vintage button to add interest and charm to your neck warmer.*

71

MATERIALS

84 assorted cotton or linen fabric squares, each 2½" × 2½" (6.5 × 6.5 cm) as follows; if buying new fabric, purchase ⅛ yd (11.5 cm) or 1 fat quarter of each color listed (the number of squares listed for each color will make a sewing machine cover like the one in the photograph, or choose your own color scheme and arrangement.)

–Red-orange (5 squares)

–Acid yellow (17 squares)

–Aqua blue (14 squares)

–Apple green (13 squares)

–Kelly green (6 squares)

–Dark green (3 squares)

–Mustard (12 squares)

–Charcoal gray (14 squares)

½ yd (45.5 cm) of 45" (114.5 cm) wide pale gray cotton fabric for background

¼ yd (23 cm) of 45" (114.5 cm) wide orange cotton fabric for binding and ties

⅞ yd (80 cm) of 45" (114.5 cm) wide cotton fabric for backing (*shown:* white with orange dots)

24" × 36" (61 × 91.5 cm) cotton batting

Coordinating thread for construction and quilting

Sturdy cardboard, such as illustration or mat board, 5" × 18" (12.5 × 45.5 cm)

TOOLS

Basic sewing tool kit (see page 15)

FINISHED SIZE

19¾" × 32" (50 × 81.5 cm) when flat

windows
SEWING MACHINE COVER

I'd always known that covering my sewing machine would help keep it clean, but I just couldn't be bothered unless the cover was worth looking at. I wanted something that would create the same feeling of joy that I get from seeing my daughter's quilt lying on her bed. I designed a simple block pattern crafted from solid-color fabrics to enhance the architecture of the machine and reinforced the top of the cover with a hidden cardboard rectangle so that it would lie firm and flat atop the machine.

→ Cut solid-colored fabrics into 2½" (6.5 cm) squares as indicated in Materials list.

→ From pale gray cotton, cut 1" (2.5 cm) wide strips the width of the fabric.

— Cut 2 of the strips into pieces 19¾" (50 cm) long for finishing the patchwork.

— Cut 2 of the strips into pieces 32" (81.5 cm) long for finishing the patchwork.

— Keep the leftovers and the remaining full-width strips for piecing the blocks.

→ Cut the orange fabric into 1½" (3.8 cm) wide crosswise strips for binding.

→ From 1 orange strip, cut four 9½" (24 cm) lengths for the ties.

→ From cotton backing fabric, cut 1 piece 30" x 40" (76 x 101.5 cm).

Making the Patchwork

All seam allowances are ¼" (6 mm). Press seams to one side, alternating sides where seams intersect.

1 | Pin 1 pale gray strip to a 2½" (6.5 cm) square, right sides together. Sew and press the seam. Trim the pale gray strip to match the square *(fig. 1)*.

2 | Pin a new pale gray strip to the pieced unit, right sides together, so that the second gray strip is perpendicular to the first. Sew and press the seam toward the new strip. Trim the gray strip to match the colored square *(fig. 2)*. Repeat Steps 1 and 2 with each colored square to make a total of 84 blocks.

3 | Sew the blocks together into 7 strips of 12 blocks each, arranging the colors as desired and alternating the placement of colored squares *(fig. 3)*.

4 | Sew the 7 pieced strips together along their long edges, as shown in the photograph on page 76, matching seams and alternating the placement of colored squares as shown in *fig. 4*, page 77, and the

Left: Side view of cover on machine; right: detail of reverse side of cover where tie is inserted between binding and backing.

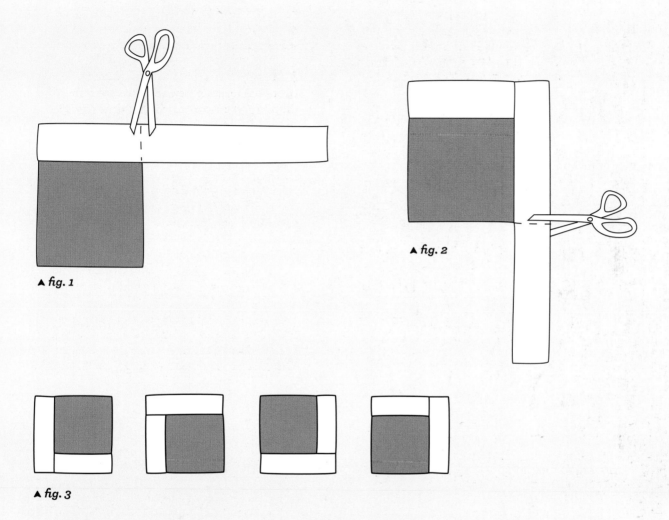

▲ fig. 1

▲ fig. 2

▲ fig. 3

photograph on page 76. This will alternate all the squares in adjacent rows for a lively, free-flowing arrangement.

5 | Pin one 19¾" (50 cm) pale gray strip to one short edge of the patchwork, right sides together. Sew and press the seam toward the strip. Repeat on the opposite short edge with the second 19¾" (50 cm) strip.

6 | Pin one 32" (81.5 cm) strip to one long edge of the patchwork, right sides together. Sew and press the seam toward the strip. Repeat on the opposite long edge with the second 32" (81.5 cm) strip.

**Basting, Quilting, and Binding
the Sewing Machine Cover**

See pages 17–33 for detailed instructions on basting, quilting, trimming, and binding.

7 | Working on a flat surface, layer the backing fabric, wrong side up, the batting, and the patchwork top, right side up.

8 | Slip the cardboard between the batting and the patchwork, positioning it behind the middle two rows of patches. The cardboard is narrower than the patchwork, so be sure to center it between the

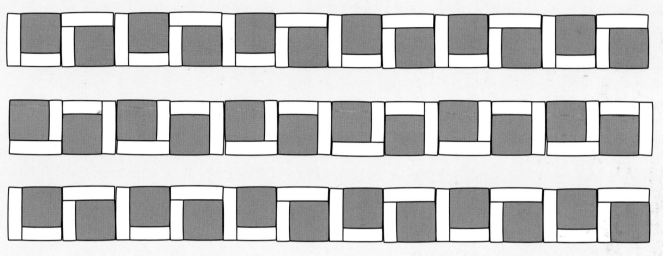

▲ *fig. 4*

long edges. With curved quilter's safety pins, pin-baste the layers together, avoiding the area with the cardboard insert. Place safety pins as close to the cardboard as possible and keep the cardboard in position by pinning the layers surrounding it with straight pins.

9 │ Machine quilt through all layers, beginning with the rows of squares on either side of the cardboard insert and working toward the ends. Remove pins as you come to them.

10 │ When the quilting is complete, trim the batting and backing even with the patchwork top. Set aside.

11 │ Press one of the 9½" × 1½" (24 × 3.8 cm) orange strips in half lengthwise, wrong sides together. Open the fabric to reveal the crease running down the middle of the strip.

12 │ Fold ¼" (6 mm) to the wrong side at one short end and press. Fold each long edge to meet the center crease and press. Refold and press once more, enclosing the raw edges on three sides.

13 │ Beginning at the raw edge, edgestitch along both long edges and across the turned-in short end.

14 │ Repeat Steps 11 through 13 to make all 4 ties.

15 │ On the back of the pieced cover, measure 6½" (16.5 cm) from the short ends on both long edges and mark. Pin a tie to each mark, aligning the raw edges, with the finished end of each tie toward the center of the cover.

16 │ Using diagonal seams, join the 1½" (3.8 cm) wide binding strips into a continuous length and bind the cover as you would a quilt, catching the tie raw edges as you stitch. I used a zigzag stitch around the perimeter of the cover to secure the binding after folding it to the back.

◄ *Opposite, top: Completed cover, front; bottom: completed cover, reverse (note that there is no quilting in area of cardboard insert).*

MATERIALS
Assorted scraps of cotton and
linen fabrics, each measuring
at least 2½" × 2½" (6.5 × 6.5 cm);
I used 6 different blue fabrics
and a small amount of mustard.

1 yd (91.5 cm) of 45" (114.5 cm)
wide natural color linen for
needle pocket and lining

½ yd (45.5 cm) of 45" (114.5 cm)
wide cotton print for inside flap
to cover needles

¾ yd (68.5 cm) of 45" (114.5 cm)
wide cotton muslin

7" × 1½" (18 × 3.8 cm) scrap
fabric strip for button loops

Coordinating thread
for construction

Contrasting thread for quilting
and topstitching (*shown:* red)

Two ¾" (19 mm) buttons

TOOLS
Basic sewing tool kit
(see page 15)

Spray starch

Rubber stamps with numerals
0 through 9 (*shown:* height of
numerals is about ¹¹⁄₁₆" [1.7 cm])

Rubber stamp inkpad for
numerals (*shown:* red)

FINISHED SIZE
15½" × 23½" (39.5 × 60 cm)
when open

indigo
NEEDLE CASE

I find that I'm forever hunting for the right knitting needles, just when I'm most excited about starting a project. That frustration inspired me to design this case for straight needles. Crafted from my favorite indigo cottons in a simple patchwork pattern, it motivates me to keep all my needles in one place. Each of the twelve needle slots is labeled to match the needle sizes, making me a model of organization. Now I just have to remember where I left the yarn . . .

→ From assorted blue scraps, cut 89 squares, each 2½" x 2½" (6.5 x 6.5 cm).

→ From mustard fabric scraps, cut 7 squares, each 2½" x 2½" (6.5 x 6.5 cm).

→ From natural linen:
– cut 1 piece 18" x 24½" (45.5 x 62 cm)
– cut 1 piece 16½" x 24½" (42 x 62 cm)

→ From cotton print fabric, cut 1 piece 15½" x 23½" (39.5 x 59.5 cm).

→ From cotton muslin, cut 1 piece 24" x 30" (61 x 76 cm).

→ Cut the scrap strip for button loops into 2 pieces, each 3½" x 1½" (9 x 3.8 cm).

Making the Patchwork

All seam allowances are ¼" (6 mm). Press all seams to one side, alternating sides where seams intersect.

1 | Arrange the patches in eight rows of 12 squares per row on a design wall or tabletop before piecing to arrive at a pleasing composition (see Making a Design Wall, page 83).

2 | Remove a single row of 12 squares from the design wall, preserving the order of the patches. Join the first 2 squares, then add the third patch in the row. Continue until all 12 patches are joined. Press all the seams to the same side.

3 | Repeat to create seven more rows of patches. Press the seams in one direction for all the odd-numbered rows and in the opposite direction for the even-numbered rows.

4 | Pin the first two rows, right sides together, along their common edge, matching the seams. The pressing directions from the previous step ensure that the seam allowances at each juncture lie in opposite directions, for easier piecing and matching the seams. Stitch and press the seam.

5 | Pin the third strip to the sewn pair, right sides together; sew and press the seam. Continue pinning, sewing, and pressing rows, one at a time, until all the rows have been sewn together.

6 | Lay the cotton muslin rectangle and the pieced patchwork, wrong sides together, on a flat surface, centering the pieced panel on the muslin. Pin-baste the layers together with quilter's curved safety pins.

7 | Machine quilt the patchwork, removing basting pins as you work. I quilted mine with straight lines spaced about ³⁄₁₆" (5 mm) apart and parallel to the long edges of the patchwork. Trim the muslin edges even with the patchwork. Set aside.

Sewing the Interior

8 | Spray both pieces of linen with spray starch and press.

9 | With wrong sides together, fold the 18" × 24½"(45.5 × 62 cm) piece in half lengthwise, to measure 9" × 24½" (23 × 62 cm), and press. This is the needle pocket.

10 | Using contrasting thread, topstitch the pocket 1"(2.5 cm) from the folded edge (I used a zigzag stitch about 2 mm wide and 2 mm long).

11 | Lay the 16½" × 24½" (42 × 62 cm) linen rectangle right side up on a flat surface. Pin the folded pocket to the larger linen rectangle, aligning the raw edges *(fig. 1)*. Machine baste in place along the bottom edge and sides.

12 | Using a removable marker, measure and mark lines 2" (5 cm) apart across the entire pocket width. The first and last lines will be 2¼" (5.5 cm) from the raw edges. Stitch along each line with contrasting thread through both the pocket and the large rectangle, beginning each stitched line at the pocket's folded edge and backstitching at the beginning and end of each line to secure the stitching and reinforce the pocket opening *(fig. 2)*.

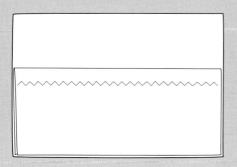

▲ *fig. 1*

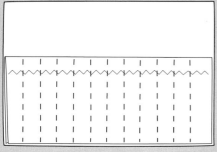

▲ *fig. 2*

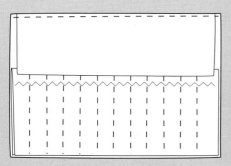

▲ *fig. 3*

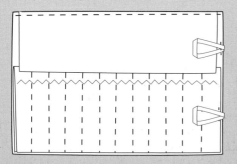

▲ *fig. 4*

Sew diagonally across corners to turn smoothly.

13 | To sew the printed fabric flap to cover the tops of the needles, fold the cotton print rectangle in half, lengthwise, with right sides together, to measure 7½" × 23½" (19.5 × 59.5 cm).

14 | Using a ¼" (6 mm) seam allowance, sew the folded fabric along the two short edges. Trim the corners diagonally and turn the cotton fabric right side out, gently smoothing the corners into place with a point turner, pencil eraser, or other blunt object. Press flat. Topstitch along the two short edges and the folded edge, ⅛" (3 mm) from the edge.

15 | With the pocket side of the needle case interior facing up, pin the assembled flap to the needle case interior along the remaining long edge, matching the raw edges and centering the flap on the linen; the flap is slightly narrower than the base *(fig. 3)*.

16 | Machine baste the flap in place ⅛" (3 mm) from the long raw edge.

▲ Stamp numbers to match knitting needle sizes.

Finishing the Needle Case

17 | Press one 3½" × 1½" (9 × 3.8 cm) button loop strip in half lengthwise, wrong sides together. Open the fabric to reveal the crease running down the middle of the strip.

18 | Fold each long edge to meet the center crease and press. Refold and press once more, enclosing the raw edges on three sides. Topstitch ⅛" (3 mm) from the long edges on both sides.

19 | Repeat Steps 17 and 18 to make the second loop.

20 | Working with one loop at a time, fold the loops in half by aligning and overlapping their raw edges. Measure and mark locations 4" (10 cm) from the top and bottom along the right edge of the needle case interior and pin a button loop to each location. Match the raw edges and position the loop folds toward the middle of the case (*fig. 4, page 81*). Machine baste the loops ⅛" (3 mm) from the raw edges.

21 | Pin the patchwork needle case exterior to the linen needle case interior, right sides together, making sure the cotton print flap and button loops are flat and their folds are not caught in the seam. Sew around the perimeter of the case, leaving a 10" (25.5 cm) opening along the edge opposite the button loops for turning.

✱TIP Sew diagonally across corners for smooth turning.

22 | Trim the corner seam allowances diagonally to reduce bulk. Turn the needle case right side out, gently working the corners into position with a point turner, pencil eraser, or other blunt object. Gently pull the loops into position and press the needle case flat, pressing the seam allowances along the 10" (25.5 cm) opening to the wrong side as you go.

23 | Slip stitch the opening in the seam. With the thread used for quilting in the needle and a color that coordinates with the linen in the bobbin, topstitch through all layers around the perimeter of the case, ⅛" (3 mm) from the edge.

24 | Working on a flat surface, lay out the needle case with the interior facing up.

25 | Rubber stamp the numbers 2, 3, 4, 5, 6, 7, 8, 9, 10, 11, 13, and 15 on the pocket slots, centering each number within its slot and positioning numbers 3" (7.5 cm) below the pocket's folded edge, as shown in the photograph. Allow the numbers to dry thoroughly.

26 | Starting at the short edge opposite the loops, roll the needle case toward the loop edge. It's a good idea to place knitting needles in a few slots before rolling to ensure the needle case is not rolled too tightly. Mark button placements on the needle case exterior and handsew the buttons in place, as shown. The button placements should be 4" (10 cm) from the long edges and about 1" (28 cm) from the loop end of the needle case.

making a *design wall*

➔ Whether the quilt is traditional, contemporary, or art, you design the elements that go into it: you audition colors, determine block placement, and consider fabric options. Making these decisions before sewing the parts together is much easier with a design wall, a felt-covered vertical surface that allows you to lay out the elements of your quilt without pinning or tacking. You can step back and see the quilt as you plan it and easily make adjustments. There are several types of design walls, ranging from permanent to portable, making it possible to add this item to your quilter's tool kit even if your space or budget is limited.

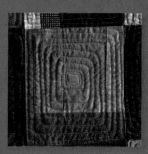

A permanent design wall is just a wall-size bulletin board covered with felt. If you've got a choice of walls you could designate as a design wall, select one that allows you to step back at least 15 to 20 feet (4.6 to 6.1 m). This will let you view the whole of your work in progress. To make a permanent design wall, I recommend covering a large sheet of Homasote board with felt or thick flannel. This board, available at lumberyards, is made from recycled paper and is most often used for soundproofing or to make temporary walls. Ask the lumberyard to cut the board to your specifications. Cover the board with white- or cream-colored felt by stretching the felt across one side of the board and securing it to the back with staples. Nail the board to the wall, and you're done. If you prefer a lighter-weight board, try Styrofoam. It too can be purchased in large sheets and cut to size.

If portability matters more than cost, purchase a freestanding portable design wall. These are available online and come in a variety of sizes ranging from 18" x 18" (45.5 x 45.5 cm) to 72" x 72" (183 x 183 cm). Prices start at less than $100. They're usually collapsible and easy to store.

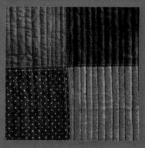

For both portability and low cost, simply tack a large sheet of felt to a wall or pin it to a curtain. Make the felt as large as you want by sewing two lengths of felt together, selvedge to selvedge. For example, if you purchase 4 yards (3.7 m) of 45" (114.5 cm) wide felt, cut it in half, and sew together the selvedge edges, you'll create a 72" x 91" (183 x 231 cm) piece (assuming that 1" [2.5 cm] will be lost in the seam). When you're done using your portable design wall, simply take it down and put it away.

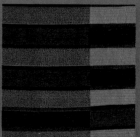

MATERIALS
Assortment of prints in a
limited color palette, half in
dark values and half in light
values, at least 6" × 8"
(15 × 20.5 cm)

¾ yd (68.5 cm) of 45"
(114.5 cm) wide white
cotton organdy

¼ yd (23 cm) of 45"
(114.5 cm) wide cotton fabric
for ties (*shown:* blue-and-
white check)

½ yd (45.5 cm) of 45"
(114.5 cm) wide cotton fabric
for borders and binding
(*shown:* white with blue dots)

White thread for machine
sewing

*Note: Scraps of the tie and
border fabrics can be used in
piecing the blocks.*

TOOLS
Basic sewing tool kit
(see page 15)

FINISHED SIZE
39½" × 29" (100.5 × 73.5 cm)

nine-patch
KITCHEN CURTAIN

Designing this kitchen curtain gave me the opportunity to combine several much-loved influences in one project. The blue-and-white palette references my favorite china, while the simple nine-patch blocks of patchwork remind me of vintage aprons. Best of all, sheer cotton organdy in the sashing and borders celebrates the magical way that the sun lights up fabric.

→ From the assortment of cotton prints, cut 135 squares, each 2½" x 2½" (6.5 x 6.5 cm). Cut either 4 or 5 squares from each print so the fabrics within a pieced block will form the pattern shown. Plan to include one light and one dark fabric in each block.

→ From cotton organdy, cut crosswise strips measuring 2" (5 cm) wide. From these strips, cut:
— 15 pieces 6½" (16.5 cm) long
— 18 pieces 8" (20.3 cm) long
— 1 piece 39½" (100.5 cm) long

→ From cotton fabric for ties, cut 18 strips, each 9¼" x 1¼" (23.5 x 3.2 cm)

→ From border fabric, cut:
— 2 pieces measuring 3½" x 39½" (9 x 100.5 cm) for upper border
— 3 crosswise strips (cut across the entire fabric width) 1½" (3.8 cm) wide for binding
— 1 piece measuring 3¼" x 39½" (8.3 x 100.5 cm) for lower border

Making the Patchwork

All seam allowances are ¼" (6 mm). Press all seam allowances to one side, alternating sides where seams intersect.

Remember that the organdy allows the seams to show through, becoming part of the curtain's appearance, so keep the seam allowances precise. Finish the seam allowances with a zigzag, overcast, or serger stitch to prevent raveling.

1 | The 9-patch blocks are assembled in three horizontal rows of 3 patches each. It's important to alternate the values of adjoining patches, so choose one light and one dark fabric for each block. The top and bottom rows in a block will be identical, with the values reversed for the center row.

2 | If the top and bottom rows are light-dark-light, the center row will be dark-light-dark.

3 | If the top and bottom rows are dark-light-dark, the center row will be light-dark-light.

4 | Arrange the fabrics for a single block beside your sewing machine. Working with 2 patches at a time, assemble the 9 patches into three rows of 3 patches. Press the seams to one side, pressing in the opposite direction for the center row.

5 | Join the strips to create the block, matching the seams, and press the seams to one side.

6 | Repeat Steps 4 and 5 to create a total of fifteen 9-patch blocks.

Attaching Organdy Borders and Sashing

7 | Pin a 6½" (16.5 cm) organdy strip to a 9-patch block, right sides together, along one edge. Sew, finish the raw edges as one, and press the seam toward the organdy (*fig. 1*).

8 | Topstitch ⅛" (3 mm) from the seam on the organdy side, sewing through all layers.

9 | Pin an 8" (20.3 cm) organdy strip to the same pieced block along an adjacent edge, so the new strip lies perpendicular to the previous organdy strip (*fig. 2*). Sew, finish the seam allowances as one, and press the seam toward the organdy.

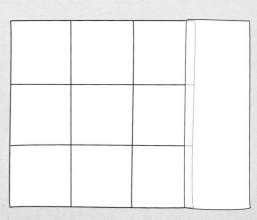

▲ *fig. 1*

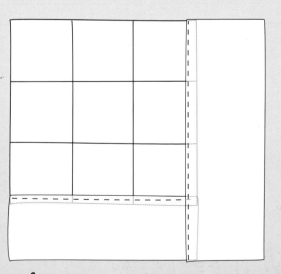

▲ fig. 2

Topstitch ⅛" (3 mm) from the seam on the organdy side, through all layers.

10 | Repeat Steps 7 through 9 to create a total of fifteen 9-patch blocks edged with organdy on two adjacent sides.

11 | Arrange all 15 blocks, right sides facing up, on a table or floor in three rows of 5 blocks each, arranging the blocks so that each is bordered by organdy along its right and bottom edges.

12 | Working from left to right on one row at a time **(fig. 3, page 88)**, pin the first 2 blocks, right sides together, pinning the organdy edge of the left block to the non-organdy edge of its neighbor. Sew, finish the seam allowances as one, and press the seam toward the organdy. Topstitch ⅛" (3 mm) from the seam on the organdy side through all layers. Replace the sewn blocks in the arrangement.

13 | Repeat Step 12 for the next 2 blocks in the row.

▲ *Crisp cotton ties give the curtain a casual look.*

87

14 | Pin the sewn pairs, right sides together, with the organdy edge of the first pair against the non-organdy edge of the second. Sew and topstitch as before.

15 | Pin the fifth block to the assembled row, right sides together, matching the non-organdy edge of the new block to the organdy edge of the assembly. Sew and topstitch as before.

16 | Pin a 6½" (16.5 cm) organdy strip to the first block in the row, right sides together, along the block's non-organdy edge *(Fig. 4)*. Sew and topstitch. This completes a row of 5 blocks, with organdy between the blocks and along both sides and the lower edge.

17 | Repeat Steps 12 through 16 to make two more rows. *Note: Row 1 is at the top of the arrangement. Row 2 is in the middle, and Row 3 is at the bottom.*

18 | Sew the rows together, in order, from top to bottom. Finish the seam allowances, press, and topstitch as before.

19 | Pin the 39½" (100.5 cm) strip of organdy to the top of Row 1, right sides together. Sew, press, and topstitch as before.

20 | Pin the bottom border piece to the bottom edge of the assembled rows, right sides together. Sew, press, and topstitch.

Making the Ties and Top Border

21 | Press ¼" (6 mm) to the wrong side along one short edge of a tie strip. Fold the strip in half, lengthwise, with wrong sides together, and press. Open the tie to reveal the center crease.

22 | Press both long edges to meet at the center crease. Refold the strip along the original crease, enclosing the raw edges, and press once more. Topstitch ⅛" (3 mm) from both long edges and the pressed-under short edge.

23 | Repeat Steps 21 and 22 to make a total of 18 ties.

24 | Divide the ties into nine pairs. Lay the ties in each pair on top of each other, raw edges matched, and treat each pair as a single unit in the next step.

25 | Lay one upper border piece on a flat surface, wrong side up. Measure and mark the tie locations as follows: the first and last ties are ½" (1.3 cm) from the side raw edges, and a third tie is precisely in the middle of the border piece. Space the remain-

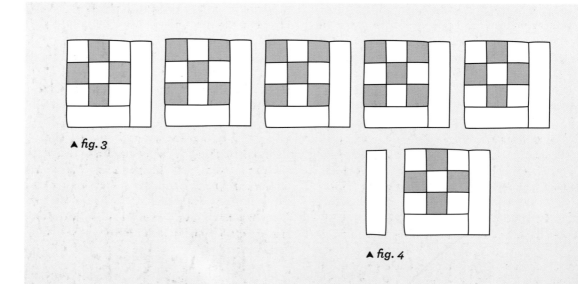

▲ fig. 3

▲ fig. 4

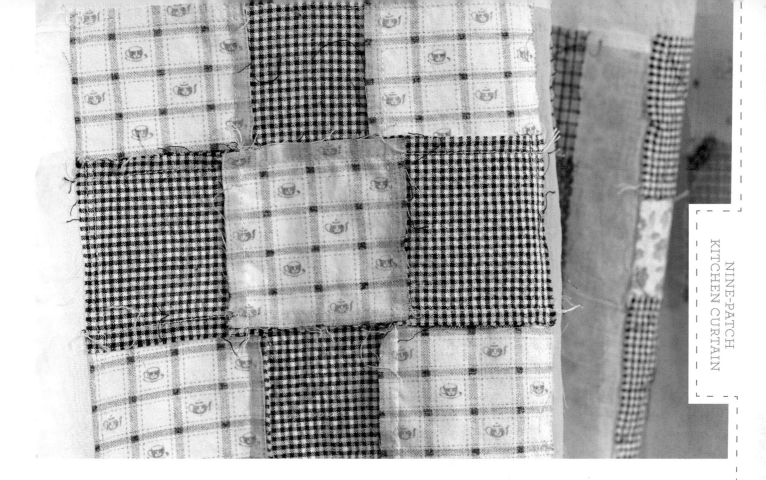

Detail of patchwork, reverse side.

NINE-PATCH KITCHEN CURTAIN

ing 6 ties about 4¾" (12 cm) apart, adjusting the locations as needed to keep the ties evenly spaced. Pin the ties in place, matching their raw edges to one long edge of the border, and machine baste ⅛" (3 mm) from the raw edge.

26 | Pin the border piece with basted ties to the other upper border piece, right sides together, making sure the ties are between the layers and lie perpendicular to the basted edge. Sew the border pieces together along the long edge with the ties. Turn the border piece right side out and press the seam open. Fold the piece in half, wrong sides together, along the seam, matching the raw edges, and press the border flat.

Finishing the Curtain

27 | Use diagonal seams to join the binding strips into a continuous length. Pin the binding to the curtain front, right sides together, along the sides and bottom edge, starting at the curtain top. Stitch.

28 | Turn the binding to the back, remembering to turn under the ¼" (6 mm) seam allowance, and pin.

29 | Using a straight or zigzag stitch, sew the binding in place, removing pins as you work.

30 | Open out the upper border so the wrong side is facing up.

31 | Press ¼" (6 mm) to the wrong side on the short edges. Press ¼" (6 mm) to the wrong side along one long edge.

32 | Pin the upper border's unfinished long edge to the curtain's top edge, right sides together. Sew, being sure to catch the short edges' pressed seam allowances in the seam.

33 | Fold the border's pressed long edge to the curtain wrong side. Match the pressed edge to the just-stitched seam and pin, covering the raw edges of the seam.

34 | Using a zigzag stitch, sew the pinned edge to the curtain back, sewing through all layers. *Note: The bobbin threads of the zigzag stitches will be visible on the curtain front.*

35 | Topstitch the upper border ⅛" (3 mm) from both short edges and the long edge with the ties.

▲ *Detail of patchwork, reverse side.*

89

MATERIALS

¼ yd (23 cm) each of 3 cotton prints in shades of brown

⅛ to ¼ yd (11.5 to 23 cm) each of 12 solid or mostly solid-colored 45" (114.5 cm) wide cottons or linens in various colors

½ yd (45.5 cm) of 45" (114.5 cm) wide cotton fabric for lining

7" (18 cm) square of coordinating cotton or linen for pocket

½ yd (45.5 cm) of 45" (114.5 cm) wide bleached or unbleached cotton muslin

Coordinating thread for construction and quilting

Pair of wooden bag handles, 12" (30.5 cm) wide with 10¼" (26 cm) slots

TOOLS

Basic sewing tool kit (see page 15)

Tracing paper

Bag template (enlarge 200%) (page 150)

Templates A + B (page 151)

Air-erasable fabric marker

FINISHED SIZE

14" (35.5 cm) at widest point, 14" (35.5 cm) tall

four points
TOTE

I designed this bag out of a desire to create patchwork yardage that could be sewn into clothing or accessories, after seeing an amazing dress one day made from a patchwork quilt. It incorporates a variety of textile influences in one project; the diamonds remind me of Kuba-cloth embroideries from Zaire, and the shape and handles are reminiscent of carpetbags. The Four Points Tote is fully lined and includes an inside pocket, making it a perfect carryall for sewing or knitting projects.

→ From brown prints, cut a total of 60 diamonds using template A. Use the rotary cutter, clear acrylic ruler, and cutting mat, or pin template to fabric and cut with scissors. With care, it's fine to cut several layers of fabric at one time.

→ From the solid and mostly solid fabrics, cut strips measuring 1½" (3.8 cm) wide and at least 8" (20.5 cm) long.

→ From the lining fabric, cut 2 bag lining pieces, using the template at the back of the book on page 150. Enlarge template to 200 percent. Fold the fabric in half crosswise and position the pattern piece on the fold near one selvedge (*fig. 1*). Pin the pattern to the fabric and cut around the pattern piece, but do not cut through the fold. Reposition the pattern along the fold in the remaining fabric, pin, and cut a second bag lining.

▲ *fig. 1*

→ From muslin, cut 2 pieces, each 18" x 22" (45.5 x 56 cm).

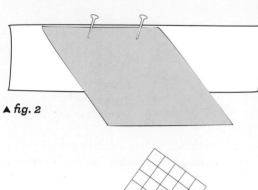

▲ *fig. 2*

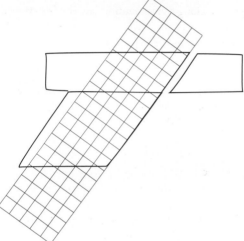

◄ *fig. 3*

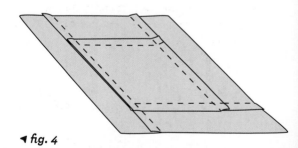

◄ *fig. 4*

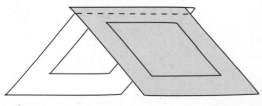

▲ *fig. 5*

Making the Diamonds

All seam allowances are ¼" (6 mm). Unless otherwise indicated, press seams to one side, alternating sides where seams intersect.

1 | Pin a 1½" (3.8 cm) strip along one side of a diamond patch, right sides together, allowing about 2" (5 cm) of the fabric strip to extend beyond each end (*fig. 2*). Sew together. Press seam away from diamond center.

2 | Lay a quilter's ruler along the small diamond edges and trim the excess strip to match (*fig. 3*).

3 | Working clockwise around the small diamond, pin a second strip of the same color along the next diamond edge, right sides together, allowing about 2" (5 cm) of the fabric strip to extend beyond each end of the pieced unit. Sew and press the seam away from the diamond center. Trim the excess strip as before.

4 | Continue pinning and sewing same-colored strips along the remaining raw edges of the small diamond, working clockwise around the diamond, until 4 strips are attached *(fig. 4)*. Press the seams away from the center diamond.

5 | Trace template B onto translucent tracing paper so the smaller diamond can be centered in the larger one before cutting.

6 | Lay the large diamond template over the assembled diamond, holding the template in place with pins or weights, and trim to fit.

7 | Repeat Steps 1 through 6 to make a total of sixty 3½" (9 cm) diamonds.

8 | Pin 2 B diamonds, right sides together *(fig. 5)*. Notice that the pieces are offset, and that the seam allowances create a V at each end of the seam. Sew and press the seam to one side. This is the first row of diamonds, indicated as Row A in the diagram *(fig. 6)*.

▲ *Detail of pieced diamonds.*

Row A
Row B
Row C
Row D
Row E
Row F
Row G

▶ *fig. 6*

9 | Continue pinning, sewing, and pressing diamonds to make the following rows: two rows of 5 diamonds (Rows B and E), two rows of 6 diamonds (Rows C and D), one row of 4 diamonds (Row F), and one more row of 2 diamonds (Row G).

10 | Referring to diagram *(fig. 6, p. 93)*, pin Rows A and B, right sides together, matching diamond points.

✱TIP To ease in matching diamond points and while rows are right sides together, poke a pin straight through the top center-diamond seam ¼" (6 mm) from the raw edge, catching the bottom patch's center-diamond seam ¼" (6 mm) from the raw edge *(fig. 7)*. Keep this pin perpendicular to the flat patches; position pins through all the layers on either side to hold the patches in place, then remove the first pin. Sew the rows together and press.

11 | Continue adding Rows C, D, E, F, and G, one at a time, referring to *fig. 6, p. 93,* for row placement.

12 | Fold the patchwork in half and pin the bag pattern piece to the patchwork, aligning the pattern's straight side with the fold. Cut the patchwork to match the paper pattern.

13 | Lay 1 muslin piece, wrong side up, on a flat surface. Lay the patchwork piece, right side up, on the muslin. Pin-baste the layers together as if to quilt.

14 | Using a walking foot attachment or using free-motion stitching, machine stitch the patchwork layer to the muslin backing by outlining the diamond shapes about ⅛" (3 mm) from the seams between blocks, removing pins as you work. Stitch on both sides of each seam, creating a stitched diamond on each pieced diamond.

15 | Repeat Steps 8 through 14 to make a second patchwork piece.

Making the Lining and Bag

16 | Using a ruler and fabric marker, make a dot on the wrong side of each long raw edge of the lining pieces, 5½" (14 cm) from the bag top. Set aside.

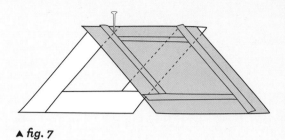

▲ *fig. 7*

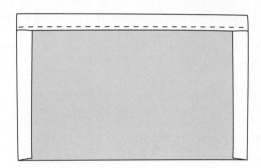

▲ *fig. 8*

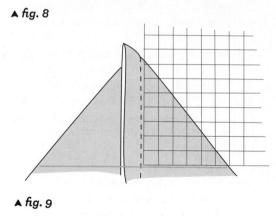

▲ *fig. 9*

17 | Stitch a ¼" (6 mm) guideline around all four sides of pocket. Press the pocket top to the wrong side along the stitched guideline.

18 | Fold a second generous ¼" (6 mm) along the pocket top to the fabric right side. Stitch across the fold along the guidelines on each side.

19 | Clip the corners to reduce bulk and turn the folded edge to the wrong side, turning the side seam allowances to the wrong side at the same time. Top-stitch near the first ¼" (6 mm) fold *(fig. 8)*.

20 | Press the remaining ¼" (6 mm) allowances to the wrong side of the side and bottom edges.

21 | Center the pocket on the right side of 1 lining piece with the pocket top edge 6½" (16.5 cm) below the bag's upper raw edge and pin. Topstitch the pocket to the lining ⅛" (3 mm) from its side and bottom edges, removing pins as you work, and leaving the top edge open.

22 | Pin the lining pieces, right sides together, beginning and ending at the dots marked in Step 1. Sew the lining pieces together from dot to dot, down the sides and across the bottom edge, backstitching at the beginning and end of stitching.

23 | Press the side seams open for 2" (5 cm), beginning at the dots.

24 | To box the bag bottom: working with one corner of the bag at a time, align the side and bottom seams to create a triangular point *(fig. 7)*.

25 | Using a quilter's clear acrylic ruler, measure 1½" (3.8 cm) along the seam from the triangle point *(fig. 9)*. With an air-erasable fabric marker, draw a line perpendicular to the seam, across the triangle from fold to fold. Stitch on the line.

26 | Repeat Steps 24 and 25 to square the second corner of the bag lining.

27 | Starting at the dots, press ¼" (6 mm) to the wrong side along all the lining raw edges. Machine baste in place. Set aside.

28 | Mark the patchwork bag pieces as directed in Step 16. Repeat Steps 22 through 27 with the patchwork bag pieces to create the bag shell.

Finishing the Bag

29 | Place the lining inside the shell, wrong sides together. Pin the shell and lining together along the machine-basted edges.

30 | Using coordinating thread and a handsewing needle, slip-stitch the bag and lining together along the basted edges. Remove the basting stitches when the slip stitching is complete.

31 | Insert one side of the bag top through the slot in 1 wooden handle, from outside to inside, pulling 1" (2.5 cm) of the bag through the slot. Pin in place. Repeat to attach the second bag side to the second handle.

32 | Slip-stitch the bag's upper edges to the lining inside the bag.

▲ *Stitch the bag's upper edges by hand to the lining after inserting the handle.*

MATERIALS
½ yd (45.5 cm) of 45"
(114.5 cm) wide cotton print
for center diamonds (*shown:*
brown with multicolored
dots)

26 assorted small pieces of
corduroy, silk, linen, or cotton
for diamonds that surround
center diamonds, each at
least 6" × 9½" (15.5 × 24 cm)
(fabrics shown include velve-
teen and an eyelet motif that
reveals the backing fabric)

½ yd (45.5 cm) of 45"
(114.5 cm) wide cotton or
linen fabric for backing
(*shown:* turquoise)

Coordinating machine sew-
ing threads for construction
and topstitching

TOOLS
Diamond template (page 152)

Basic sewing tool kit
(see page 15)

FINISHED SIZE
8" × 55" (20.5 × 139.5 cm)

mix-it-up patchwork
SCARF

There's something special about wearing something that you've made yourself. It's empowering to be able to clothe yourself by your own efforts. A scarf isn't an absolute essential, but it takes away the chill on a cold day. And what better way to warm your neck than with a fabulous patchwork scarf crafted from a variety of fabrics and textures? Wear this scarf and chances are high that others will notice and compliment you—and you can proudly say, "I made it myself." Go ahead—mix it up!

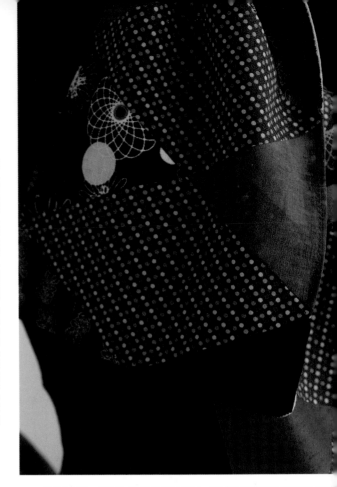

cutting the **fabric**

→ Trace or photocopy the diamond template to make a paper pattern. Secure the pattern to the fabric with pins or weights and cut around the pattern with a rotary cutter or scissors. The template includes seam allowances.

→ From the center diamond fabric, cut 12 diamonds.

→ From assorted corduroy, silks, linens, and cottons, cut 26 diamonds.

→ From backing fabric, cut 2 pieces, each measuring 8½" x 28" (21.5 x 71 cm).

Making the Patchwork

All seam allowances are ¼" (6 mm). Press seams to one side, alternating sides where seams intersect.

1 | Pin 1 center diamond and 1 assorted-fabric diamond, right sides together, along one edge *(fig. 1)*. Notice that the pieces are offset, and that the seam allowances create a V at each end of the seam. Sew along the pinned edge and press the seam to one side.

2 | Pin another assorted-fabric diamond to the pair, right sides together *(fig. 2)*, along the center diamond edge opposite the first seam. Sew along the pinned edge and press the seam.

3 | Repeat Steps 1 and 2 to make a total of 12 strips of 3 diamonds each.

Top: Detail of patchwork. Bottom: Detail of reverse side of scarf with zigzag topstitching all around.

4 | Pin 2 diamond strips, right sides together, along a long edge, easing as needed to match the seams of the center-diamond points where they cross, ¼" (6 mm) from the raw edges (along the new seamline) *(fig. 3)*. Note that the first diamond in the bottom strip adjoins a raw edge of the top strip's central diamond. When joined, the rows have zigzagging side edges. Sew and press.

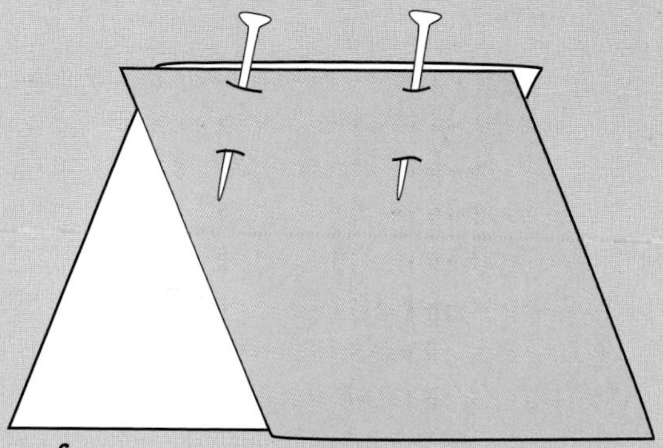

▲ fig. 1

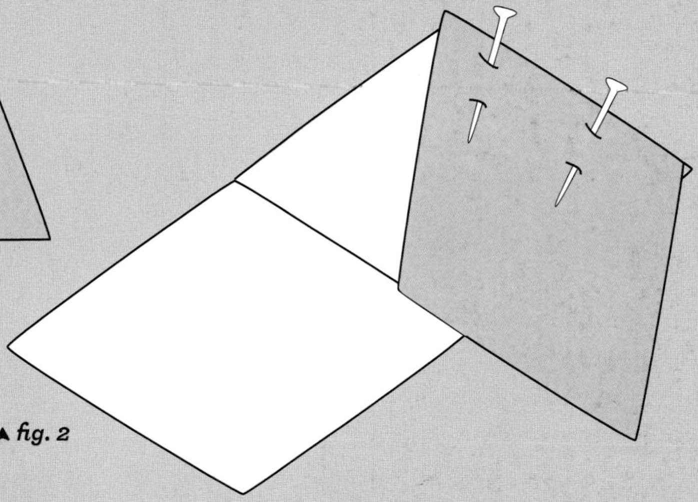

▲ fig. 2

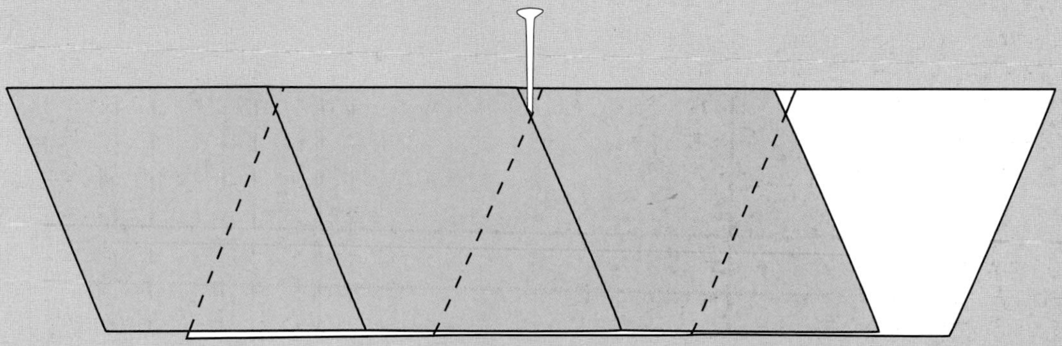

▲ fig. 3

5 | Attach the remaining strips, one at a time.

6 | Add 1 diamond patch to the empty corner of each short edge. Place the new diamond on the free edge of the center diamond, right sides together. Sew and press the seams.

7 | Using a rotary cutter, clear acrylic ruler, and cutting mat, trim the short ends of the scarf to make a straight edge. Position the ruler ¼" (6 mm) above the seamline junction at the point of the center diamond, keeping it perpendicular to the center of the scarf (imagine a line running through the center diamonds' centers) **(fig. 4, p. 101)**.

The Mix-It-Up
Patchwork Scarf
*will brighten
any wardrobe.*

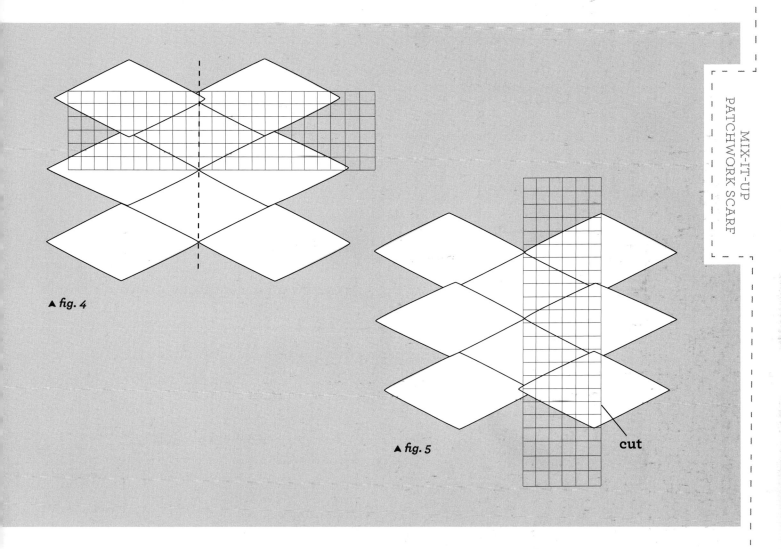

▲ fig. 4

▲ fig. 5

cut

8 | Using a rotary cutter, clear acrylic ruler, and cutting mat, trim the long edges of the scarf to make a straight edge. Position the ruler ¼" (6 mm) outside the seamline junction at the points of the center diamonds, keeping it parallel to the center of the scarf *(fig. 5)*.

Finishing the Scarf

9 | Sew the two backing fabric sections together along one short edge. Press the seam open.

10 | Pin the scarf to the backing, right sides together. Sew around all edges, leaving a 10" (25.5 cm) opening in one long edge for turning the scarf right side out.

11 | Trim the corners to reduce bulk and turn the scarf right side out. Press the edges, turning the seam allowance along the opening to the wrong side as you go. Pin the opening closed.

12 | Using a zigzag stitch (2.0 mm wide and 2.0 mm long) and coordinating thread, stitch around the scarf perimeter, ⅛" (3 mm) from the edge, removing the pins along the opening as you come to them. I used different thread colors in the needle and bobbin to match both sides of the scarf.

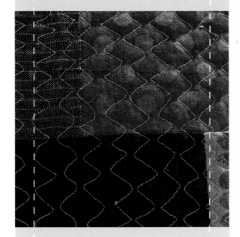

MATERIALS

⅛ yd (11.5 cm) of 45"
(114.5 cm) wide or wider
wool or linen menswear
suiting fabric

⅛ yd (11.5 cm) each of four
45" (114.5 cm) wide light-
colored linen or cotton
fabrics

⅛ yd (11.5 cm) each of two 45"
(114.5 cm) wide dark-colored
linen or cotton fabrics

¾ yd (68.5 cm) of 45"
(114.5 cm) wide cotton muslin

⅝ yd (57 cm) of 45"
(114.5 cm) wide cotton
corduroy for backing

¼ yd (23 cm) of 45" (114.5
cm) wide coordinating fabric
for binding (*shown:* magenta
douppioni)

24" × 24" (61 × 61 cm)
cotton batting

Coordinating thread for
construction and quilting

18" (45.5 cm) or longer
polyester zipper

TOOLS
Basic sewing tool kit
(see page 15)

FINISHED SIZE
18" × 18" (45.5 × 45.5 cm)

menswear
PILLOW

When I first started to sew, I
thought there were hard and fast
rules about what kinds of fabrics
could be sewn together. I finally
came to realize that unconventional
mixing of different weights and
textures could produce beautiful
items. This liberating idea is the
inspiration for the Menswear
Pillow. A graphic pattern and
limited palette allowed me to mix
fabrics as disparate as linen suiting,
Japanese ikat, contemporary cotton, silk douppioni, and corduroy.

→ From menswear suiting fabric, cut and label 9 Menswear A pieces measuring 2½" x 3½" (6.5 x 9 cm) (*shown:* black/gray stripe).

→ From each of 2 light-colored fabrics (fabrics 1 and 2), cut and label 3 Light B pieces measuring 6½" x 3½" (16.5 x 9 cm) (*shown:* black/white stripe and multicolor dots).

→ From each of the other 2 light-colored fabrics (fabrics 3 and 4), cut and label 3 Light A pieces measuring 2½" x 3½" (6.5 x 9 cm) (*shown:* yellow prints).

→ From 1 dark-colored fabric (fabric 5), cut 3 Dark B pieces measuring 6½" x 3½" (16.5 x 9 cm) (*shown:* orange).

→ From remaining dark-colored fabric (fabric 6), cut 6 Dark C pieces measuring 4½" x 3½" (11.5 x 9 cm) (*shown:* maroon).

→ From cotton muslin, cut 1 piece 24" x 24" (61 x 61 cm).

→ From corduroy backing fabric, cut 2 pieces, each measuring 19" x 12" (48.5 x 30.5 cm), with the ribs parallel to the 19" (48.5 cm) edge.

→ Cut the binding fabric into 1½" (3.8 cm) wide crosswise strips.

Making the Pillow Top

All seam allowances are ¼" (6 mm). Unless otherwise indicated, press seams to one side, alternating sides where seams intersect. When pressing corduroy, iron on the wrong side to prevent flattening the pile. Lay a scrap of corduroy or a thick towel face up on the ironing board under the piece being pressed to cushion the nap.

1 | Pin 1 Menswear A to each Light B, right sides together, along a 3½" (9 cm) edge. Sew together and press the seam to one side.

2 | Pin each sewn pair with Light B fabric 1 to a pair containing Light B fabric 2, right sides to-gether, along one short edge, so that the Menswear A patch of one pair is pinned to the Light B patch of the second pair. Sew and press.

3 | Pin a new Menswear A patch to each sewn strip, right sides together, matching the new Menswear A patch to the free edge of a Light B patch. Sew and press. The result is strips alternating Menswear A and Light B patches (*fig. 1*). Label these strips A and set aside.

4 | Pin a Dark C to each Light A, right sides to-gether, along one 3½" (9 cm) edge. Sew and press.

5 | Pin a Dark B to each Light A fabric 3 patch, right sides together, along the free 3½" (9 cm) edge. Sew and press.

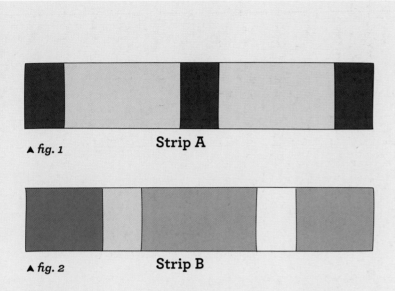

▲ *fig. 1*   **Strip A**

▲ *fig. 2*   **Strip B**

A

B

A

B

A

B

▲ *fig. 3*

6 | Pin a unit from Step 5 to each of the remaining pairs from Step 4, right sides together, so that the Dark B rectangle is between the Light A patches (*fig. 2*). Sew and press. Label these strips B.

7 | Pin one A strip to one B strip, right sides together, along one long edge. Sew and press. Repeat to make a total of three pairs of strips. Refer to the construction diagram (*fig. 3*) and the project photo for fabric arrangement.

8 | Pin two strip pairs, right sides together, along one long edge, making sure the A and B strips alternate. Sew and press.

9 | Add the third sewn strip pair to the first two, making sure the A and B strips alternate.

**Basting, Quilting, and
Finishing the Pillow Top**

See pages 17–33 for detailed instructions on basting, quilting, trimming, and binding.

10 | Layer the cotton muslin (wrong side up), cotton batting, and pillow top (right side up) on a flat surface. Pin-baste the layers together with quilter's curved safety pins.

11 | Machine or handquilt as desired. I machine quilted my pillow top with an overall pattern of wavy lines. You can accomplish this effect with free-motion quilting or by using a decorative stitch pattern on your sewing machine. Remove the curved pins as you sew.

12 | Trim the layers to match the pieced pillow top.

13 | Using diagonal seams, sew together enough binding strips to equal at least 76" (193 cm). Set aside.

14 | Insert the zipper between the backing panels (see Inserting a Zipper into Pillow Backing, at

Left: Detail of patch-work and quilting; right: zipper inserted into pillow backing.

right). Make sure the corduroy nap runs in the same direction on both pieces.

15 | Working on a table covered with a self-healing cutting mat, layer the zippered pillow back (wrong side up) and quilted pillow top (right side up). Pin the pillow top to the backing. Partially open the zipper so the zipper pull lies within the perimeter of the pillow top. Trim the backing so it is flush with the pillow top.

16 | Sew the binding to the pillow edges through all layers, removing pins as you work, and being careful to avoid the metal stops at the zipper top and bottom.

inserting a zipper into a pillow backing

→ *I often use zippers in my pillow backings to make the forms removable, allowing me to replace flattened forms quickly and keep the pillow looking full. To craft a backing with a lapped (covered) zipper, begin with a polyester zipper at least the length or width of the pillow. For example, if your pillow measures 18" (45.5 cm) square, you need an 18" (45.5 cm) or longer zipper. Trimming a zipper is as simple as cutting off any unneeded length; when trimming, be sure to keep the zipper pull within the boundaries of the project so it isn't accidentally cut off and discarded. You can easily sew across the teeth of a polyester zipper and cut it with a rotary cutter or scissors. Follow these easy steps:*

1

Cut 2 pieces for the pillow back, making sure each is as tall as the pillow and at least 3" (7.5 cm) wider than half the pillow width.

2

Press 1¼" (3.2 cm) to the wrong side along one long edge of a pillow back.

3

Pin the closed zipper to the prepared backing with the zipper right side against the pressed hem allowance. Align the top of the zipper tape with the top edge of the fabric and position the zipper tape edge ¼" (6 mm) from the raw edge of the pillow back hem *(fig. 1)*. The folded hem will completely cover the zipper from the right side.

4

Attach a zipper foot to your machine; the zipper foot allows the needle to be positioned very close to the zipper teeth and can also be positioned to sew to the right or left of the zipper teeth. Begin stitching on the zipper tape at the bottom end of the zipper, about ⅛" (3 mm) from the edge of the zipper tape. The stitches will both attach the zipper and secure the hem and will be about 1" (2.5 cm) from the pressed fold. Stitch toward the zipper pull, removing pins as you reach them, and stop 3" to 4" (7.5 to 10 cm) from the pull. Do not cut the thread.

5

Lower the needle, raise the presser foot, and slide the zipper pull past the presser foot and into the previously sewn region. Lower the presser foot and finish sewing the zipper tape to the pillow back. By moving the zipper pull out of the way, you avoid creating a "bump" of stitching where the presser foot is pushed out of line by the bulky zipper pull.

6

Press ¼" (6 mm) to the wrong side along one long edge of the second pillow back. With right sides facing up, pin the pressed edge to the unstitched zipper tape, placing the fold close to the zipper teeth. Place the assembly on the sewing machine bed with the zipper pull and the previously sewn back panel to the left of the zipper foot. Fold the previously sewn hem out of the way. Begin sewing at the open end of the zipper, with the zipper pull still positioned lower on the zipper.

7

Sew a few inches, stopping short of the zipper pull. Lower the needle and raise the presser foot. Slide the zipper closed, lower the presser foot, and sew to the end of the zipper tape *(fig. 2)*.

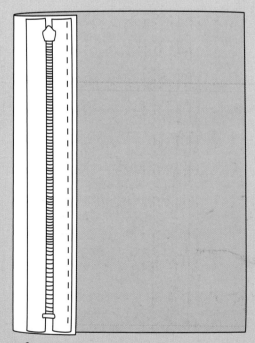

▲ *fig. 1*

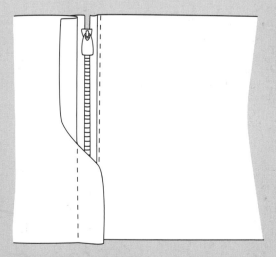

▲ *fig. 2*

MATERIALS

20 assorted cotton and linen fabric pieces, solid-colored or mostly solid, each at least 6" × 10" (15 × 25.5 cm), for book pages

24 assorted cotton and linen fabric pieces in a variety of prints and colors, each at least 7" × 7" (18 × 18 cm), for appliquéd letters

⅝ yd (57 cm) of 45" (114.5 cm) wide cotton print fabric for page breaks, binding, and ties

¾ yd (68.5 cm) of 45" (114.5 cm) wide cotton print fabric for book backing

¼ yd (23 cm) fusible interfacing

½ yd (45.5 cm) fusible web

1 yd (91.5 cm) cotton batting

Coordinating thread for construction and quilting

TOOLS

Basic sewing tool kit (see page 15)

Pinking shears or pinking blade for rotary cutter

FINISHED SIZE

closed: 9¾" × 9¾" × 1½" (25 × 25 × 3.8 cm)

fully open: 9¾" × 78" (25 × 198 cm)

ABC
BABY BOOK/ CRIB BUMPER

This alphabet book challenged me to find a way to include all of the letters of the alphabet in its eight pages. I planned this book to be multifunctional: folded and tied along one edge it is a beautiful book for you and your baby to flip through, touch, and explore; open, it can be tied to the slats of a crib as a bumper. I used twenty different fabrics in reds, yellows, blues, oranges, and greens for the book pages and twenty-four prints in an array of colors for the appliquéd letters.

→ From the solid and mostly solid fabrics, cut:
— Twenty 5" x 5" (12.5 x 12.5 cm) squares
— Six 5" x 9½" (12.5 x 24 cm) rectangles

→ From the page break/binding/tie fabric, cut 12 strips 1½" (3.8 cm) x the fabric width. From those strips, cut:
— Fourteen 9¾" x 1½" (25 x 3.8 cm) page-break strips
— Twelve 9" x 1½" (23 x 3.8 cm) strips
— 5 complete strips to create binding about 5½ yd (503 cm) long

→ From backing fabric, cut eight 11" x 11" (28 x 28 cm) squares. Tip: If your fabric runs a bit narrow, cut the pieces 10½" x 11" (26.5 x 28 cm). Because the backings will be trimmed to size, the smaller dimensions will still work.

→ From fusible interfacing, cut fourteen 9¾" x 1½" (25 x 3.8 cm) strips.

→ From cotton batting, cut eight 11" x 11" (28 x 28 cm) squares.

Making the Pages

All seam allowances are ¼" (6 mm). Press seams to one side, alternating sides where seams intersect.

1 | Pin two 5" × 5" (12.5 cm × 12.5 cm) squares, right sides together, along one edge. Sew and press the seam. Repeat with a second pair of squares.

2 | Pin both pairs, right sides together, along one long edge, matching the center seam. Sew together and press the seam.

3 | Repeat Steps 1 and 2 to make a total of three 4-patch pages.

4 | Pin two 5" × 5" (12.5 cm × 12.5 cm) squares, right sides together, along one edge. Sew and press. Pin the sewn pair to one 9½" × 5" (24 × 12.5 cm) rectangle, right sides together, along one long edge. Sew and press.

5 | Repeat Step 4 to make a total of 4 pages, each consisting of 2 squares and 1 rectangle.

6 | Pin two 9½" × 5" (24 × 12.5 cm) rectangles, right sides together, along one long edge. Sew and press, making 1 page consisting of 2 rectangles.

Adding the Letters

*Note: All letters are cut freehand using pinking shears or a rotary cutter fitted with a pinking blade. Combine upper- and lower-case letters as desired. My letters measure about 4" (10 cm) tall and 4" (10 cm) wide. Some letters were cut directly from fabric; others were constructed from cut strips. For example, the letter A was constructed from 3 strips, cut with pinking shears, and then fused to the page to form the A shape (**fig. 1**).*

7 | Arrange your pages in the order desired.

8 | Following the manufacturer's instructions, apply fusible web to the back of 1 print scrap. Using an air-erasable fabric marker, draw the shape of a letter on the fabric right side. It may be helpful to sketch a 4" × 4" (10 × 10 cm) square on the fabric before starting to better visualize the finished letter size. Letters placed on rectangular patches can be a bit wider.

9 | Using pinking shears or a rotary cutter with a pinking blade, cut out the letter shape. Peel away the paper backing.

10 | Fuse the letter to a square or rectangle in the appropriate spot on the pages, keeping to alphabetical order (**fig. 2**).

11 | For letters composed of straight lines, freehand cut strips 1" to 1¾" (2.5 to 4.5 cm) wide with the pinking shears or blade, if desired. Arrange the strips on a background patch, trimming their length as necessary, and fuse in place.

12 | Repeat the two methods until all letters are cut and fused to their pages.

Free-motion quilting loosely follows the pinked edges of the letters.

13 | Topstitch the letters about ⅛" (3 mm) inside the pinked edges.

14 | Working on a hard, flat surface, layer 1 backing fabric square, wrong side up; 1 batting square; and 1 page with fused letters, right side up. Pin-baste the layers together with quilter's curved safety pins.

15 | Free-motion quilt around the outline of each letter following the curvy pinked edges, as shown in the photograph at left, remembering to remove basting pins as you work.

16 | Trim the layers so that all edges are even. Repeat for the remaining pages.

Putting the Pages Together

17 | Fuse an interfacing strip to the back of each page-break strip.

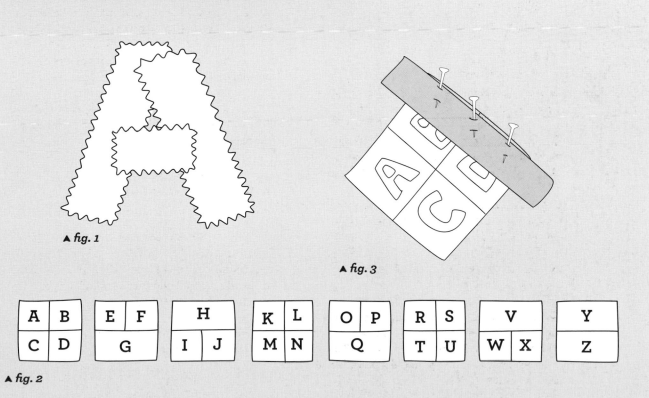

▲ *fig. 1*

▲ *fig. 3*

▲ *fig. 2*

Completed
book folded
and tied.

▶ fig. 4

▼ fig. 5

18 | Working with the first page (A-B-C-D) facing up, pin a page-break strip to the right-hand side of the page, right sides together (*fig. 3, p. 111*). Pin a second page-break strip to the back of the page along the same edge, right sides together.

19 | Sew the page-break strips to the page's right-hand edge, sewing through all layers (front page-break strip, quilted page, and back page-break strip). Press both strips away from the book edge and edgestitch close to the seam.

20 | Press ¼" (6 mm) to the wrong side along the long raw edges of both page-break strips.

21 | Slide the left-hand edge of the next page between the pressed edges of the page-break strip. The pressed edges overlap the new page ¼" (6 mm) (*fig. 4*). Pin the strips to the page front and back. Edgestitch close to the pressed edges through all layers to secure the new page.

22 | Repeat Steps 18 through 21 to add each page, one at a time, sewing the page-break strips to the right-hand edge of the square added during the previous sequence.

Finishing the Book

See pages 31–33 for detailed instructions on binding method.

23 | Working on an ironing surface with one 9" × 1½" (23 cm × 3.8 cm) strip at a time, press ¼" (6 mm) to the wrong side along one short edge.

24 | Fold the strip in half, lengthwise, with wrong sides together, and press. Open to reveal the center crease. Fold and press both long edges to meet the center crease.

25 | Refold the strip along the center crease and press again. Edgestitch the folded tie along both long edges and the pressed short edge.

26 | Repeat Steps 23 through 25 to create 12 ties.

27 | Referring to the diagram (*fig. 5*), position the prepared ties in pairs with their raw edges abutting the book raw edges. At each location, there will be one tie on the back of the book/bumper and one on the front. Ties along the first and last pages should be placed along the page side, 1" (2.5 cm) from the top and bottom corners, lying parallel to the book/bumper's long edges. Place the center ties at the center top and bottom of the fourth page-break strip, perpendicular to the long edges.

28 | Pin the ties in place, with raw edges matched and the bulk of each tie lying over the book itself, and machine baste ⅛" (3 mm) from the raw edges. Pin the ties' finished ends out of the way so they aren't caught in the stitches to follow.

29 | Using diagonal seams, sew the binding strips together, forming a continuous length. Attach the binding to the book/bumper as you would to a quilt. Be sure to catch all the ties' raw edges in the stitches.

30 | Fold the binding to the back of the book/bumper and pin, remembering to fold under ¼" (6 mm) seam allowance. Using a machine zigzag stitch, sew through all the book and binding layers. As you zigzag, fold the ties pinned to the first and last pages *away* from the book and sew over them in this position.

31 | To tie the book into an accordion shape, place the last page right side down so its ties fall along the left side. Accordion-fold each page. Using the ties, secure the first and last pages along the left-hand edge. The ties at the book's center remain loose inside the book, available when the project is used as a bumper and tied to the crib rails.

fresh quilts
for wall, bed + baby

→ A FRIEND ONCE TOLD ME that despite the fact that she makes art quilts, she likes knowing that she could still wrap herself in those quilts on a cold winter night. I love that idea; it speaks to what makes a quilt, in some ways the simplest of sewn creations, so special. Whether a quilt is meant to decorate a wall, grace a table, or wrap a newborn baby, it can simultaneously beautify and warm. Crafting something as essential as a covering, yet one that is fresh, modern, and beautiful, is the underlying concept behind the quilt designs in this section. My goal was to create quilts that fit into a contemporary setting, embracing a modern palette and simplified shapes, yet still speaking of comfort and protection. I hope they'll inspire you to gather your fabric bits and stitch together a quilt that will delight your eyes and warm your body, even if it originally was meant to hang on a wall.

MATERIALS

Cotton and linen in 30 to 35
different prints and solids;
use scraps or purchase ⅛ yd
(11.5 cm) or 1 fat quarter (18"
× 22" [45.5 × 56 cm]) of each
fabric

½ yd (45.5 cm) of 45"
(114.5 cm) wide cotton print
for center hexagons and half-
hexagons (center)

⅝ yd (57 cm) each of 2
different natural-colored
45" (114.5 cm) wide cottons
or linens (background)

1⅜ yd (125.5 cm) of 45"
(114.5 cm) wide cotton fabric
for backing

¼ yd (23 cm) of 45"
(114.5 cm) wide cotton or
linen fabric for binding

45" × 45" (114.5 × 114.5 cm)
cotton batting

Coordinating thread for
construction and quilting

TOOLS

Basic sewing tool kit
(see page 15)

Templates A, B, C, D, E, F
(pages 155–156)

Pattern paper or tracing
paper

Masking tape to secure quilt
for pin-basting

Quilter's safety-pin
fastening tool (optional)

FINISHED SIZE

34" × 36" (86.5 × 91.5 cm)

modern
BABY QUILT

Baby quilts are a joy to piece and
quilt, because their size means
nearly instant gratification. They're
wonderful to give, too, because they
don't have to fit, they don't need to
match the nursery, and when the
baby is no longer a baby, they can
hang on a wall. Best of all, a beautifully crafted baby quilt is a shoo-in
to become an heirloom. This design
mixes fun, contemporary fabrics
and a traditional technique of sewing Y-shaped seams to create a quilt
for totally modern babies.

→ See page 19 for instructions about using templates. If a pattern used repeatedly becomes worn along the edges, make a new pattern from the original template to preserve accuracy.

→ From scraps of cotton or linen prints and/or solids, cut 108 pieces using template A.

→ From center fabric, cut:
— 7 pieces using template B
— 4 pieces using template C

→ From background fabrics, cut the following, using each fabric for about half of the pieces:
— 54 pieces using template A
— 50 pieces using template D
— 8 pieces using template E
— 12 pieces using template F

→ Cut the backing fabric to 45" x 45" (114.5 x 114.5 cm).

→ From the binding fabric, cut four 1½" (3.8 cm) wide strips across the fabric width.

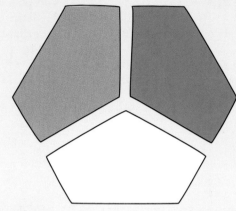

▲ *fig. 1*

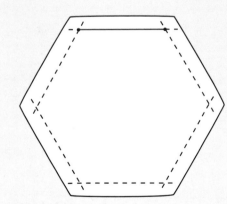

▲ *fig. 2*

Piecing the Quilt Top

All seam allowances are ¼" (6 mm). See information on piecing Y seams, page 25.

1 | Gather 2 prints and a background fabric cut from template A *(fig. 1)*. Pin and stitch the 3 pieces with a Y seam. Press seams to one side. Repeat to make a total of 6 "petals," each containing 2 prints and 1 background piece.

2 | Pin a petal to one edge of a center hexagon, right sides together, along one straight edge, matching the edge with 2 print fabrics to the center hexagon side. Stitch, beginning and ending the seam ¼" (6 mm) from the raw edges, at the point where the intersecting seamlines cross *(fig. 2)*. Do not press seams.

3 | Align a petal piece with the V made by the 2 pieces in Step 2, right sides together, setting up a

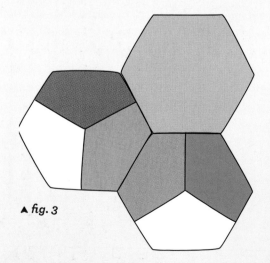

▲ *fig. 3*

new Y seam with one leg already sewn. Starting ¼"
(6 mm) from the outside corner, between the 2 petals, stitch to the junction with the center hexagon;
backstitch to secure the seam. Stitch the third
arm of the Y, joining the new petal to the center
hexagon, stopping ¼" (6 mm) from the hexagon raw
edges. Backstitch to secure the seam. You now have
2 petals attached to the center hexagon *(fig. 3)*.

4 | Repeat Steps 2 and 3 to attach 4 more petals
around the center hexagon. The last petal will have
three sides to sew rather than 2. Press the seams
away from the central hexagon. You now have a
"flower" consisting of a central hexagon with 6
petals *(fig. 4)*.

5 | Repeat Steps 1 through 4 to make a total of 7
flowers.

6 | Create a hexagon block from each flower by
adding 6 D background pieces *(fig. 5)*. Join each D
to the flower with the Y piecing technique, this time
sewing all the way to the block's outer edge.

*Begin your quilting in the center of the hexagon with a spiral,
then follow the lines of the hexagon as you sew.*

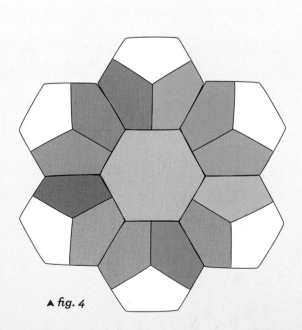

▲ *fig. 4*

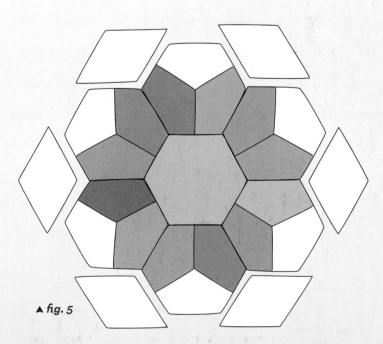

▲ *fig. 5*

Modern Baby Quilt

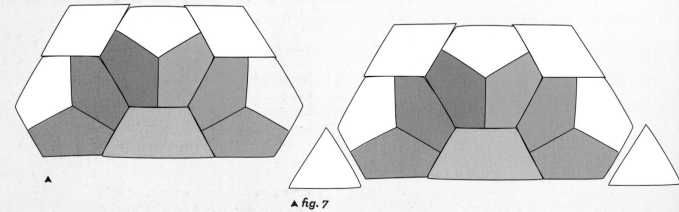

▲ *fig. 7*

7 | Press the diamond seams toward the hexagon center.

8 | Make a total of 7 hexagon blocks.

9 | To make half-hexagon blocks, begin by making 3 petals. Sew these to a C patch, with the petal prints adjoining the half-hexagon. Attach 2 D background pieces between the petals *(fig. 6)*.

10 | With right sides together, pin and sew an E triangle to each side of the half-hexagon block to complete it *(fig. 7)*. Press the seams toward the half-hexagon center.

11 | Repeat Steps 9 and 10 to make a total of 4 half-hexagon blocks.

12 | To assemble the quilt top, arrange the hexagon blocks and half-hexagon blocks as shown in the photograph and *fig. 8*.

13 | The blocks not in the center row are squared by adding F triangles. As shown in *fig. 8*, sew an

F triangle to each half-hexagon block. Sew 2 F triangles to adjacent sides of hexagon blocks 3, 4, 6, and 7.

14 | Starting with the center row of hexagon blocks, pin Block 1 to Block 2, right sides together, along their common edge. Beginning ¼" (6 mm) from the corner, stitch the blocks together, stopping ¼" (6 mm) short of the next corner.

15 | Referring to Steps 2 through 4, considering each pieced hexagon block as a petal and Block 1 as the center, join the remaining hexagon blocks, one at a time.

16 | Working in the corner formed by Blocks 2 and 7, pin a half-hexagon (Block 8) to the main quilt body, right sides together. Join, using the Y piecing technique, and continuing the seam along the short edge of the F triangle to the edge of the quilt. Press the seams toward the central half-hexagon of the block. Repeat to attach the other 3 half-hexagon blocks, one at each corner of the quilt.

Basting, Quilting, and Finishing the Quilt

See pages 17–33 for detailed instructions on basting, quilting, trimming, and binding the quilt.

17 | Layer the quilt backing (wrong side up) on a flat work surface. Smooth the fabric outward from the center and secure it by taping the backing edges to the work surface with masking tape. The backing should be taut but not stretched. Smooth on the batting, then the quilt top (right side up), centering the quilt top on the other layers. Pin-baste the layers together with quilter's curved safety pins.

18 | Hand or machine quilt as desired. I quilted spirals in each center hexagon and half-hexagon, as well as in the hexagons formed by D patches in adjacent blocks. I also quilted about ¼" (6 mm) inside each petal and around each flower formed by adjacent petals.

19 | Stitch the binding strips together, using diagonal seams, and attach the binding to the quilt.

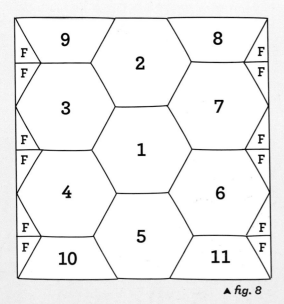

▲ *fig. 8*

MATERIALS

In selecting fabrics for this quilt, limit the overall color and value palette, but include a few squares of intense color to brighten the quilt top.

Assorted cottons and linens in a wide variety of prints and solids, each scrap measuring at least 4" × 4" (10 × 10 cm)

4 yd (3.7 m) of 45" (114.5 cm) wide cotton fabric for backing

½ yd (45.5 cm) of 45" (114.5 cm) wide cotton or linen fabric for binding

68" × 68" (170 × 170 cm) cotton batting

Coordinating threads for construction and quilting

TOOLS

Basic sewing tool kit (see page 15)

10½" (26.7 cm) diameter plate

Masking tape to secure quilt for pin-basting

Quilter's safety-pin fastening tool (optional)

FINISHED SIZE

60" × 60" (152.5 × 152.5 cm)

annie's
PICNIC QUILT

The design for this picnic quilt was inspired by the amazing textile work of Bauhaus artist Annie Albers. Her beautiful weavings celebrate simple shapes and limited color palettes, yet the patterns seem complex and different every time I encounter them. A quilt destined for picnics should be easy to make, but capable of revealing new patterning even when you spill potato salad on it. Use a few of the quilt fabrics to make a set of the World's Easiest Napkins, page 125, and you're ready to go!

→ Cut 289 assorted cotton and linen squares, each 4" x 4" (10 x 10 cm).

→ Cut the backing fabric into 2 pieces, each 72" (183 cm) long.

→ Cut 11 bias strips, each 1½" (3.8 cm) wide, from the binding fabric.

Making the Patchwork

All seam allowances are ¼" (6 mm). Press seams to one side, alternating sides where two seams meet. Before piecing, arrange the squares on a design wall (see page 83) or on the floor to audition placement of different fabrics.

▶ *Top: Annie's Picnic Quilt; bottom: simple outline quilting emphasizes the pieced squares.*

1 | Beginning at the upper left corner and preserving the arrangement from the design wall, pin 2 4" (10 cm) squares right sides together along one edge and stitch. Join the third square to the first 2, then add the fourth square. Continue across the horizontal row, assembling 17 squares to make the first row. Press the seams to one side. Return the row to the design wall.

2 | Sew the patches in the second row together. Press the seams in the direction opposite the first row's seams. Return the row to the design wall.

3 | Continue down the patchwork arrangement, assembling each row of 17 patches. Alternate the seam pressing so each odd-numbered row is pressed in one direction and each even-numbered row is pressed the opposite way.

4 | Pick up the first two assembled rows and place them right sides together, matching all the seamlines. Stitch the rows together and press the seam toward the second row.

5 | Join the third row to the first two, matching all the seamlines, and press the seam toward the third row.

6 | Continue assembling the rows from the top of the layout to the bottom, matching all the seams and pressing the seam allowances downward, to complete the quilt top.

Basting, Quilting, and Finishing the Quilt

See pages 17–33 for detailed instructions on basting, quilting, trimming, and binding the quilt.

7 | Remove the selvedges from the backing fabric pieces. Pin the 2 pieces, right sides together, along one long edge. Stitch the backing pieces together and press the seam open.

8 | Lay the assembled backing, wrong side up, on a flat surface. Smooth the fabric outward from the center and secure it by taping the backing edges to the work surface with masking tape. The backing should be taut but not stretched. Smooth the batting over the backing, then center the quilt top, right side up, on the other layers.

9 | Pin-baste the quilt sandwich together.

10 | Using a coordinating machine-quilting thread and a darning foot (for free-motion quilting) or a walking foot (for machine-guided quilting) on your sewing machine, machine quilt the quilt sandwich. I quilted my top with lines of stitches ¼" (6 mm) to each side of every seam.

11 | Trim the backing and batting to match the quilt top.

12 | Round the corners of the quilt by positioning the 10½" (26.5 cm) dinner plate face down along the corners. With a fabric marker, trace the rounded edge. Use a rotary cutter or scissors to trim the corners along the marked lines through all layers.

13 | Use diagonal seams to sew the binding strips together, making one continuous length. Pin and stitch the binding to the quilt, right sides together, remembering to ease the binding along the rounded edges.

14 | Fold the binding to the back side of the quilt and pin, enclosing the raw edges and turning under ¼" (6 mm) of the binding raw edge as you work.

15 | Using thread to match the binding in both the needle and the bobbin of your sewing machine, stitch the binding in place with a zigzag stitch.

▼ *World's easiest napkins, in fabrics to match quilt.*

world's easiest *napkins*

I haven't had this confirmed by the folks from The Guinness Book of World Records, *but I'm pretty sure these are the most easily made napkins known to humanity. For each napkin, you'll need 2 washed fat quarters, a sewing machine, and about five minutes of time. Whip them up and head out on your picnic.*

1
Remove the selvedges from 2 fat quarters. Pin the fat quarters right sides together.

2
Stitch around the perimeter of the fabrics in a ¼" (6 mm) seam, using the smaller fat quarter as a guide if the two are uneven. Leave a 3" (7.5 cm) unstitched opening for turning and remove the pins as you stitch.

Turn stitched fabrics right side out and press edges, gently poking out corners with a point turner or other blunt tool.

4
Turn in ¼" (6 mm) seam allowance at the opening and press.

5
On outside edges of napkin, topstitch ⅛" (3 mm) around all four sides, including the opening.

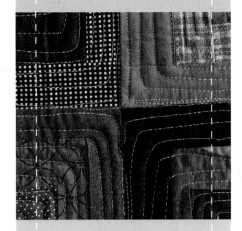

MATERIALS

36 cotton and linen fabric scraps, each at least 2" × 2" (5 × 5 cm); half should be warm-colored prints and solids, half cool-colored prints and solids.

Cotton and linen strips, each at least 1½" × 4" (3.8 × 10 cm), for a total of about 2 yards (1.8 meters) of fabric; half should be warm-colored prints and solids, half cool-colored prints and solids.

1½ yd (112 cm) of 45" (114.5 cm) wide cotton or linen fabric for backing

½ yd (45.5 cm) of 45" (114.5 cm) wide cotton or linen fabric for binding

Cotton batting, 45" × 45" (114.5 × 114.5 cm)

Coordinating thread for construction and quilting

TOOLS

Basic sewing tool kit (page 15)

Masking tape

Quilter's safety-pin fastening tool (optional)

FINISHED SIZE

36" × 36" (91.5 × 91.5 cm)

nate's
QUILT

I've made this design several times, and I never tire of it. Improvisational piecing makes each incarnation different and engaging, but the rules of fabric selection and construction remain the same. This is a perfect project for practicing freehand rotary cutting and a go-with-the-flow approach to piecing. Collect a variety of fabric scraps in warm colors (reds, oranges, yellows, warm pinks, and browns) and cool colors (greens, blues, purples) for this quilt.

→ From the 18 warm-colored scraps, freehand-cut 18 squares, ranging in size from 2" x 2" (5 x 5 cm) to 5" x 5" (12.5 x 12.5 cm). Use a rotary cutter, self-healing cutting mat, and quilter's ruler, and consider the dimensions here only as a guide. Don't worry if your squares are not exact in size or shape.

→ From the 18 cool-colored scraps, freehand-cut 18 squares, ranging in size from 2" x 2" (5 x 5 cm) to 5" x 5" (12.5 x 12.5 cm), as directed above.

→ From the binding fabric, cut 4 strips, each 1½" (3.8 cm) wide, across the fabric from selvedge to selvedge.

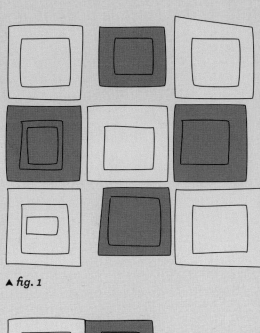

▲ *fig. 1*

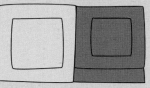

▲ *fig. 2*

Making the Patchwork

All seam allowances are ¼" (6 mm). Press seams to one side, alternating sides where seams intersect.

Aim for a finished block size of 6" × 6" (15 × 15 cm) to achieve the 36" × 36" (91.5 × 91.5 cm) finished quilt size. The quilt top is made of four sections of 9 blocks each. Two have 5 cool blocks and 4 warm blocks, and two have 5 warm blocks and 4 cool blocks, arranged to alternate warm and cool. Make one 9-block section at a time.

1 | Pin a cool-colored strip to one edge of a cool-colored square, right sides together. Stitch and press the seam. Trim the strip length to match the square.

2 | Pin a second cool strip to the square, right sides together, perpendicular to the first strip. Stitch, press the seam, and trim.

3 | Continue pinning, sewing, pressing, and trimming a third and fourth strip so that the center cool square is surrounded by cool strips. Repeat these steps to make a total of 5 blocks in cool colors.

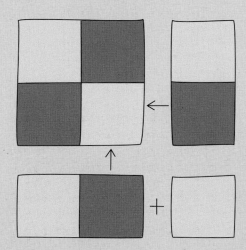

▲ *fig. 3*

Nate's Quilt

4 | Repeat Steps 1 through 3, substituting warm-colored squares and strips, to make a total of 4 blocks in warm colors.

5 | On a table or design wall (see Making a Design Wall, page 83), arrange the blocks so that cool and warm blocks alternate. Move blocks around to create an arrangement that pleases you *(fig. 1)*.

6 | Move the first 2 blocks, one cool and one warm, from the layout to the sewing machine. Because the squares are cut freehand and will not be uniform in size, you may need to add strips to make the common edges equal in length. Pin the blocks, right sides together, along their common edge. Stitch and press the seam, and trim the larger block if necessary *(fig. 2)*. Return the block to the layout.

7 | Referring to your layout, repeat Step 6 with the pair of blocks adjacent to the first pair, adding strips if needed. Pin, stitch, and press the seam. Trim if necessary.

8 | Sew the first and second block pairs together along their common long edge, adding strips if needed. Press the seam and trim if necessary. Return the unit to the layout.

9 | Repeat Steps 7 and 8 to join a third pair of blocks and add it to the previous group of 4, adding strips or trimming if necessary. Six of the 9 patches for the first 9-patch block are now sewn together.

10 | Pin, stitch, and press the remaining 3 blocks into a strip. Pin the 3-block strip and the 6-block

▲ *Detail of improvisational piecing and free-motion quilting. Contrasting binding adds to the vibrancy of the quilt.*

group, right sides together, along their common long edge *(fig. 3)*. Stitch, press the seam, and trim if necessary. You now have a 9-block section with alternating warm- and cool-color blocks.

11 | Repeat Steps 1 through 10 to make a second section with 5 cool and 4 warm blocks. Repeat the steps twice more to make two sections with 5 warm and 4 cool blocks.

12 | On a design wall or floor, arrange the four 9-block sections, alternating the two types of sections. Referring to your layout, pin two 9-block sections, right sides together, along one edge. Add strips of fabric to the sections if needed to equalize lengths. Stitch, press the seam, and trim the larger section if necessary. Repeat with remaining pair of 9-block sections to yield two 18-block sections.

13 | Pin the two 18-block sections, right sides together, along their common edge. Stitch and press the seam, trimming if necessary.

Basting, Quilting, and Finishing the Quilt

See pages 17–33 for detailed instructions on basting, quilting, trimming, and binding the quilt

14 | Lay the backing fabric, wrong side up, on a flat surface. Smooth the fabric outward from the center and secure it by taping the backing edges to the work surface with masking tape. The backing should be taut but not stretched. Layer the batting over the backing and then add the quilt top, right side up, centered on the other two layers. Pin-baste the layers, using quilter's curved safety pins and a fastening tool such as Kwik Klip, if desired.

15 | Quilt by hand or machine, as desired. I quilted concentric squares with rounded corners about ¼" (6 mm) apart on many blocks, using straight lines, wavy lines, or a combination. For other blocks, I quilted back and forth across the width of the strips.

16 | Trim the backing and batting to match the quilt top and ensure that the quilt corners are square.

17 | Using diagonal seams, sew the binding strips together. Attach the binding by machine and handstitch the binding to the quilt back, remembering to turn the ¼" (6 mm) seam allowance to the wrong side.

10

ways to ♥ *improvisational piecing*

→ *Piecing a quilt top improvisationally should be a liberating experience. Yet, for many sewers, experienced or otherwise, the thought of freehand cutting and piecing causes them to hyperventilate rather than breathe easy. If you're one of these quilters, before you reach for a brown paper bag, consider these ten helpful hints to make improvisation groovy, not grating.*

1

Relax. Ruining a piece of fabric is not the worst mistake you can make in life.

2

Trust your eyes. Put away your measuring tools and freehand-cut a few 4" x 4" (10 x 10 cm) squares. Now measure these squares. You'll be surprised how close you get to the desired measurement.

3

Add or delete fabric as needed. Take comfort in the fact that if a block is not the same size as its neighbor, you can adjust the size by adding or cutting away an extra strip or two.

4

Embrace wonkiness. The energy of improvisational pieces comes from the fact that the parts are slightly— or more than slightly—off-kilter. If you want that quality, improvisation is the way to go.

5

Squaring off is always an option. If you like the energy of off-kilter pieces, but want to contain it, know that at any point in the creation of a top you can use a quilter's clear ruler, cutting mat, and rotary cutter to square off the edges.

6

Size disparity is a good thing. Making blocks *sans* measuring tools can yield blocks of varying sizes. Use this visual element to your advantage by making additional blocks in a variety of sizes; then, by adding or deleting fabric strips, fit the blocks together like puzzle pieces.

7

Accentuate the edges. Improvisational piecing often yields a quilt with edges that aren't quite straight. Highlight this design feature by easing binding along angled or curved edges rather than straightening them out. If your edges are especially curvy, cut the binding strips on the bias for more stretch.

8

Contain the energy with sashing strips. If you like the energy of individual blocks but want to tone it down a bit, add wide vertical and/or horizontal strips of solid-colored fabric between the blocks to give the eye some visual rest. This can also help organize seemingly disparate blocks into a cohesive quilt top.

9

Utilize color. Improvisationally pieced blocks and color go well together. Bright, intense hues accent the energy of these blocks. Don't be timid in your color choices.

10

Focus on solids. An improvisationally pieced quilt doesn't benefit from the use of lots of printed and patterned fabric; vivid colors and piecing give it plenty of intensity. Narrow your fabric choices to solids and prints that read as mostly one color.

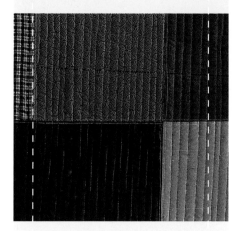

MATERIALS

3 yd (2.75 m) total of cotton, linen, and/or silk douppioni fabrics in cool colors such as blue, green, gray, and greenish-yellow (color group A), each piece measuring at least 8½" × 16" (21.5 × 40.5 cm).

3 yd (2.75 m) total of cotton, linen, and/or silk douppioni fabrics in warm colors such as red, orange, reddish purple, and warm shades of brown (color group B), each piece measuring at least 8½" × 16" (21.5 × 40.5 cm).

5⅝ yd (5.2 m) coordinating 45" (114.5 cm) wide fabric for backing

½ yd (45.5 cm) coordinating 45" (114.5 cm) wide fabric for binding

66" × 96" (167.5 × 244 cm) cotton batting

Coordinating threads for construction and quilting

If using silk douppioni, 2 yd (183 cm) lightweight fusible interfacing or enough to back each silk rectangle

TOOLS

Basic sewing tool kit (see page 15)

Masking tape to secure quilt for pin-basting

Quilter's safety-pin fastening tool (optional)

FINISHED SIZE

60" × 90" (152.5 × 228.5 cm)

whirlygig
QUILT

This quilt is based on a very simple block—two rectangles joined along a common long edge that are then sewn perpendicular to a similar pair of rectangles. The scale of the rectangles and thoughtful use of mostly solid-colored fabrics give the quilt plenty of impact, and the blocks are large, so they go together quickly. Striking from a distance, this quilt also beckons you to look more closely with its varied textures and colors.

→ From color group A, cut 24 rectangles measuring 8" x 15½" (20.5 x 39.5 cm).

→ From color group B, cut 24 rectangles measuring 8" x 15½" (20.5 x 39.5 cm).

→ From the backing fabric, cut three 66" (167.5 cm) lengths and remove the selvedges.

→ From the binding fabric, cut eight 1½" (3.8 cm) wide crosswise strips.

→ If using silk douppioni, cut a rectangle of light-weight fusible interfacing measuring 8" x 15½" (20.5 x 39.5 cm) for each silk fabric rectangle.

Making the Patchwork

All seam allowances are ¼" (6 mm). Press the seams open unless otherwise directed.

1 | If using silk douppioni rectangles, fuse light-weight interfacing to the wrong side of each, following the manufacturer's instructions.

2 | Pin one rectangle from color group A to one rectangle from group B, right sides together, along one long edge. Sew, press the seam open, and top-stitch ⅛" (3 mm) from the seam along both sides. Repeat to make a total of 24 blocks, each comprising 2 rectangles *(fig. 1)*.

3 | Pin 2 of the blocks from Step 2, right sides together, so that the rectangles in one block are perpendicular to the rectangles in the second block. Sew, press, and topstitch ⅛" (3 mm) from the seam along both sides. Repeat to make a total of twelve 4-rectangle units *(fig. 2)*.

4 | Pin 2 of the 4-rectangle units, right sides together, so that adjacent rectangle pairs are perpendicular and the warm-colored (group B) fabrics create a whirligig pattern *(fig. 3)*. Sew, press, and topstitch as before. Repeat to make a total of six 8-rectangle units.

5 | Pin 2 of the 8-rectangle units, right sides together, and sew, keeping the whirligig pattern

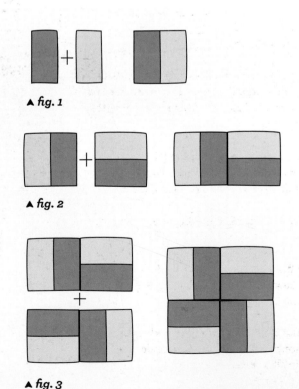

▲ fig. 1

▲ fig. 2

▲ fig. 3

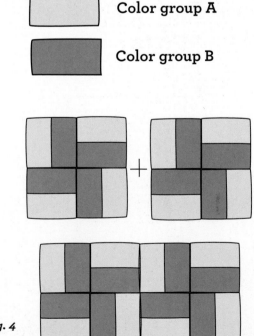

Color group A

Color group B

▶ fig. 4

(*fig. 4*). Press the seam open and topstitch as before. Repeat to make a total of three 16-rectangle sections.

6 | Pin two 16-rectangle sections, right sides together, along one long edge. Sew, press, and top-stitch. Pin the third 16-rectangle section to the first two, right sides together, along one long edge. Sew, press, and topstitch (*fig. 5*).

Basting, Quilting, and Finishing the Quilt

See pages 17–33, for detailed instructions on basting, quilting, trimming, and binding the quilt.

7 | Join the three backing fabric sections along their long edges with ¼" (6 mm) seams to create a backing 66" (167.5 cm) wide and about 125" (317.5 cm) long. Press the seams open.

8 | Smooth the backing fabric, wrong side up, on a flat work surface. Smooth the fabric outward from the center and secure it by taping the backing edges to the work surface with masking tape. The backing

Whirlygig Quilt

should be taut but not stretched. Layer the batting and then the quilt top, right side up and centered on the other layers. Pin-baste the layers together with curved safety pins.

9 | Hand or machine quilt as desired. I machine quilted mine with stitches spaced about ½" (1.3 cm) apart and running vertically along the quilt.

10 | Trim the backing and batting layers to match the quilt top.

11 | Using diagonal seams, sew the binding strips together to create a continuous length. Sew the binding to the quilt.

12 | Fold the binding to the quilt's back and slip-stitch in place, remembering to turn under the ¼" (6 mm) seam allowance.

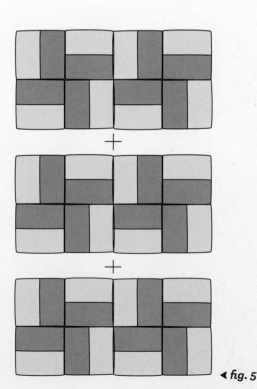

◄ fig. 5

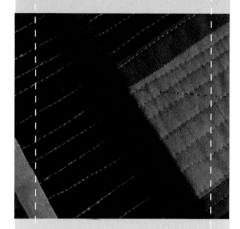

MATERIALS

1 yd (91.5 cm) of 45" (114.5 cm) wide cotton, Color A (Rose)

1 yd (91.5 cm) of 45" (114.5 cm) wide cotton, Color B (Dark Blue)

¾ yd (68.5 cm) of 45" (114.5 cm) wide cotton, Color C (Acid Green)

1 yd (91.5 cm) of 45" (114.5 cm) wide cotton, Color D (Red)

⅞ yd (80 cm) of 45" (114.5 cm) wide cotton, Color E (Greenish Blue)

⅝ yd (57.5 cm) of 45" (114.5 cm) wide cotton, Color F (Pale Blue)

⅝ yd (57.5 cm) of 45" (114.5 cm) wide cotton, Color G (Mustard)

½ yd (45.5 cm) of 45" (114.5 cm) wide cotton, Color H (Purple)

¼ yd (23 cm) of 45" (114.5 cm) wide cotton, Color I (Dark Green)

½ yd (45.5 cm) of 45" (114.5 cm) wide cotton, Color J (Chartreuse)

⅜ yd (34 cm) of 45" (114.5 cm) wide cotton, Color K (Charcoal)

51½" × 53" (131 cm × 134.5 cm) cotton batting

Coordinating thread for construction and quilting

TOOLS

Basic sewing tool kit (see page 15)

Masking tape

Quilter's safety-pin fastening tool (optional)

FINISHED SIZE

43½" × 45" (110.5 × 114.5 cm)

strips + stripes
QUILT

When the design of this quilt felt clean and elegant and spare, I knew it was right. To maintain that simplicity, I did something unusual for me—I pieced the entire top and back out of newly purchased richly hued shot cottons from the Kaffe Fassett collection. You don't have to use the same fabrics I did, but sticking to one brand of solids will enhance the minimalist nature of this quilt.

→ From Color A, cut:
- 6 strips 14¾" x 1" (37.5 x 2.5 cm) for top
- 4 rectangles 7½" x 30" (19 x 76 cm) for back
- Cut the remaining fabric into 1½" (3.8 cm) wide crosswise-grain binding strips

→ From Color B, cut:
- 5 rectangles 14¾" x 3" (37.5 x 7.5 cm) for top
- 2 rectangles 15" x 30" (38 x 76 cm) for back

→ From Color C, cut:
- 2 rectangles 14¾" x 3" (37.5 x 7.5 cm) for top
- 6 strips 14¾" x 1" (37.5 x 2.5 cm) for top
- 4 rectangles 4" x 30" (10 x 76 cm) for back
- Cut the remaining fabric into 1½" (3.8 cm) wide crosswise-grain binding strips

→ From Color D, cut:
- 7 rectangles 14¾" x 3" (37.5 x 7.5 cm) for top
- 10 strips 14¾" x 1" (37.5 x 2.5 cm) for top
- 4 rectangles 4" x 30" (10 x 76 cm) for back
- Cut the remaining fabric into 1½" (3.8 cm) wide crosswise-grain binding strips

→ From Color E, cut:
- 3 rectangles 14¾" x 3" (37.5 x 7.5 cm) for top
- 4 rectangles 5" x 30" (12.5 x 76 cm) for back

→ From Color F, cut:
- 10 rectangles 14¾" x 3" (37.5 x 7.5 cm) for top
- Cut the remaining fabric into 1½" (3.8 cm) wide crosswise-grain binding strips

→ From Color G, cut:
- 5 rectangles 14¾" x 3" (37.5 x 7.5 cm) for top
- 10 strips 14¾" x 1" (37.5 x 2.5 cm) for top
- Cut the remaining fabric into 1½" (3.8 cm) wide crosswise-grain binding strips

→ From Color H, cut:
- 3 rectangles 14¾" x 3" (37.5 x 7.5 cm) for top
- 6 strips 14¾" x 1" (37.5 x 2.5 cm) for top
- Cut the remaining fabric into 1½" (3.8 cm) wide crosswise-grain binding strips

→ From Color I, cut:
- 6 strips 14¾" x 1" (37.5 x 2.5 cm) for top
- Cut the remaining fabric into 1½" (3.8 cm) wide crosswise-grain binding strips

→ From Color J, cut:
- 7 rectangles 14¾" x 3" (37.5 x 7.5 cm) for top

→ From Color K, cut:
- 3 rectangles 14¾" x 3" (37.5 x 7.5 cm) for top
- 4 strips 14¾" x 1" (37.5 x 2.5 cm) for top

Making the Patchwork

All seam allowances are ¼" (6 mm). Press seams to one side, alternating sides where seams meet.

The quilt top is assembled in nine sections, which are arranged in three horizontal rows and three vertical columns. Within each column there is a single main color that is used in all three sections. Within each row, all 3 blocks are the same size and arrangement, although their colors differ.

1 | To create the sections in the top row, beginning with the top left section, pin one 14¾" × 1" mustard (G) strip to one 14¾" × 3" purple (H) rectangle, right sides together, along a long edge. Sew and press the seam. *Note: All the strips in this section are color G, and the contrasting rectangles are color H.*

2 | Pin a second G strip to the opposite long edge of the same H rectangle, right sides together. Sew and press.

3 | Pin a pale blue (F) rectangle to the sewn unit, right sides together, along one long edge of a G strip. Sew and press. The F rectangle is now the bottom of the unit. *Note: The F rectangles are the main color in the left column and will be used in all three of its sections.*

4 | Repeat Steps 1 through 3 to create three sections of H and F rectangles with G strips between them. Sew these three sections together so a G strip is at the top and an F rectangle is at the bottom. Remember to press all the seams as you go. This completes the top section of the left column.

5 | Using **fig. 1** and quilt photograph on page 140 as a color guide, repeat Steps 1 through 4 to make the top sections of the middle and right columns. For the center column, use red (D) strips, pale blue (F) as the contrasting rectangles, and chartreuse (J) as the main color that appears throughout the center column. To create the right column, use acid green (C) strips, mustard (G) as the contrasting rectangles, and red (D) as the main color throughout the column.

6 | The sections in the middle row are smaller than the top sections. For the middle section of the left column, pin and sew a red (D) strip to a mustard (G) rectangle. Sew a second D strip to the other long edge of the G piece, then sew an F rectangle to the second D strip. Repeat to make one more unit.

7 | Sew the two units from Step 6 together to complete the middle left section. There will be a D strip at the top and an F rectangle at the bottom.

8 | Repeat Steps 6 and 7 to create the other two middle sections, referring to **fig. 1** and photograph to confirm color placement. For the center middle section, use mustard (G) strips, dark blue (B) as the contrast, and continue with chartreuse (J) as the main color. For the right middle section, the colors are charcoal (K) for the strips and acid green (C) for the contrast, with red (D) continuing as the main color for the right column.

9 | The bottom sections are larger than the middle ones and have strips at both the top and the bottom. Remember that the main-color rectangles always alternate with the contrast-color rectangles in a column. To piece the bottom left section, begin by pinning and sewing a rose (A) strip to a dark blue (B) contrast rectangle. Next, add a second A strip to the other side of the B rectangle. Sew a pale blue (F; main color) rectangle to the assembled unit.

10 | Repeat Step 9 to make a second unit, then sew the two units together with the contrast and main rectangles alternating.

Diagonal seams or straight seams can join the multicolored binding strips.

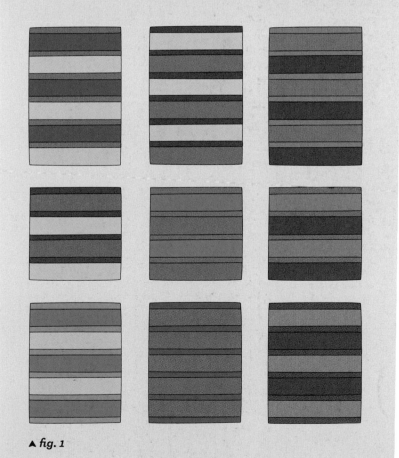

▲ *fig. 1*

Strips and Stripes Quilt

11 | Sew an A strip to the free edge of the bottom F rectangle, then attach another B rectangle to the A strip. To complete the section, sew an A strip to the last B rectangle's free edge. Remember to press all the seams.

12 | Repeat Steps 9 through 11 to construct the bottom sections for the other two columns. Use purple (H) strips, charcoal (K) contrast rectangles, and chartreuse (J) main-color rectangles for the second column. The third column's bottom section uses dark green (I) strips, greenish blue (E) contrast rectangles, and red (D) main rectangles.

13 | Using *fig. 1* and photograph at left to double-check color placement, sew the three sections of each column together. Remember that a narrow strip falls between each pair of rectangles, and that the main- and contrast-color rectangles alternate throughout each column.

14 | Pin the three columns together, matching seams, as shown in the construction diagram and quilt photograph. Sew and press the seams.

Making the Quilt Backing

15 | Sort the 30" (76 cm) wide backing pieces into pairs. You will have one pair of dark blue (B) pieces and two pairs each of A, C, D, and E.

16 | Pin a pair of pieces together along one short edge. Stitch the seam and press it to one side.

17 | Repeat Step 16 with each remaining pair.

18 | Following *fig. 2*, arrange the stitched backing rectangles with the wide dark blue (B) rectangle in the center and the other colors above and below it: rose (A), acid green (C), red (D), and greenish blue (E). Pin the long edges of the first 2 backing strips together. Sew and press the seam. Add backing strips, one at a time, sewing and pressing seams, until the backing is complete.

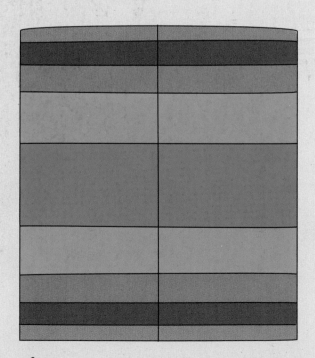

▲ *fig. 2*

Basting, Quilting, and Binding the Quilt

See pages 17–33 for detailed instructions on basting, quilting, trimming, and binding the quilt.

19 | Lay the pieced backing, wrong side up, on a flat surface. Smooth the fabric outward from the center and secure it by taping the backing edges to the work surface with masking tape. The backing should be taut but not stretched. Make sure the seams are perpendicular to the vertical seam in the center so the strips will be parallel to the quilt edges when finished. Smooth the cotton batting on the backing, then add the quilt top, right side up. Center the quilt top on the backing so equal amounts of the E rectangles in the backing will be visible in the finished quilt and keep the quilt top's edges parallel to the backing edges and seams. Pin-baste the layers together with quilter's curved safety pins, using a tool such as Kwik Klip to close the pins if desired.

20 | Machine or handquilt as desired. I quilted with free-form straight lines, spaced from ¼" to ⅝" (6 mm to 1.5 cm) apart, across the whole of the quilt.

21 | Trim the edges of the backing and batting flush with the quilt top.

22 | Examine the binding strips and plan the position of each binding section to match a color in the adjacent quilt top block.

23 | Begin with the binding for the center block at the bottom of the quilt. Pin the matching binding to the quilt top with its short end extending ¼" (6 mm) beyond the block seam. Sew the binding to the quilt, beginning 3" (7.6 cm) from the short end and stopping 3" (7.6 cm) from the next block seam. Trim the seam binding ¼" (6 mm) beyond the block seam.

24 | Join the next binding color (the one that matches the corner block) to the first with a ¼" (6 mm) seam. The binding seam should align with the quilt top seam. Pin and sew the binding to the quilt, beginning at the end of the previous stitching and continuing around the corner. Miter the binding at the corner and sew to a point 3" (7.5 cm) before the next block seamline.

25 | Join the third binding color to the second. Continue attaching the binding around the entire quilt, stopping to add new colors at each seamline.

26 | When you arrive back at the starting point, trim the final color ¼" (6 mm) beyond the last block seam and sew it to the raw edge of the first color, then stitch the last few inches (cm) of the binding to the quilt. Complete the binding.

27 | If you prefer diagonal seams as shown on the sample quilt, allow extra fabric to extend beyond the seam at the beginning and add each new binding section using the method for finishing a binding on page 32.

creating your own color scheme

→ **AS SHOWN**, this quilt uses a total of eleven different colors of shot cotton by designer Kaffe Fassett. The top uses all eleven colors, the backing uses five colors, and the pieced binding uses seven colors.

→ **TO ASSEMBLE** your own color combination, plan on ½ yard (45.5 cm) for each color in the quilt top, 1 yard (91.5 cm) for two of the backing colors and ½ yard (45.5 cm) for three of the backing colors, and ⅛ yard (11.5 cm) of each color in the binding. So, for example, if a color is used in all three places, you'll purchase 1⅛ to 1⅝ yards (103 to 148.5 cm) of each color.

→ **ANOTHER** option is to follow the yardages listed on page 137, substituting your own colors for those in the sample. For convenience, each is identified by a letter as well as a color name; simply make a chart of the letters with your chosen colors and use it as a guide for purchasing, cutting, and piecing the quilt.

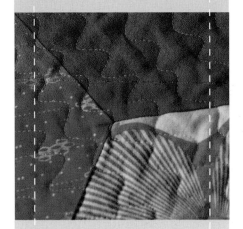

MATERIALS

1½ yd (137 cm) of 45"
(114.5 cm) wide white or
cream cotton or linen for
hexagons and binding

¼ to 1 yd (23 to 91.5 cm) each
of 22 different 45"
(114.5 cm) wide cotton or
linen prints in shades of acid
yellow, acid green, gray, and
warm yellow for hexagons

5 yd (4.6 m) of 45" (114.5 cm)
wide coordinating fabric for
backing

Full/queen size package
cotton batting

Coordinating thread for construction and quilting

TOOLS

Hexagon Quilt templates A,
B, and C (pages 153–154)

Basic sewing tool kit
(see page 15)

Masking tape to secure quilt
for pin-basting

Quilter's safety-pin
fastening tool (optional)

FINISHED SIZE

75" × 82" (190.5 × 208 cm)

honeycomb hexagon
QUILT

To reinterpret the traditional hexagon-based Grandmother's Flower Garden quilt design in a fresh, contemporary way, I enlarged the usually tiny hexagon patch for a finished size of 6½" (16.5 cm) from side to side, limited the color palette, mixed in plenty of white and cream tones, and arranged the hexagons randomly rather than organizing them into flowers. Although the quilt is a departure from tradition, the resulting pattern reminds me of honeycombs, so a lovely connection to the garden remains.

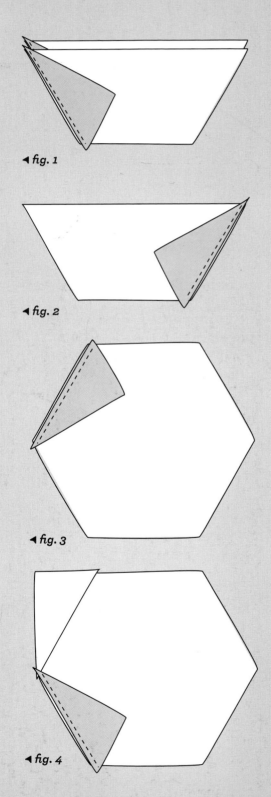

→ From white or cream cotton or linen fabric, cut:
- 28 hexagons using template A
- 3 half-hexagons using template B
- 8 right triangles using template C
- 9 crosswise strips 1½" (3.8 cm) wide for binding

→ From the 22 assorted cotton or linen prints, cut:
- 128 hexagons using template A
- 10 half-hexagons using template B
- 42 right triangles using template C
  (Note: Cut 40 of the right triangles as pairs, using the same fabric for each pair. This allows you to pair them along the edges, where they will appear as hexagon segments.)

→ Cut the backing fabric into two 90" (229 cm) lengths and remove the selvedges.

Making the Patchwork

All seam allowances are ¼" (6 mm). Press seams to one side, alternating sides where seams intersect. Refer to page 25 for information regarding the Y piecing technique.

Making the Left and Right End Rows

1 | Pin 1 half-hexagon (B) and 1 triangle (C), right sides together, matching C's longest edge to B's left edge *(fig. 1)*. The longest edge of C will appear longer than the side of B, but the seamlines are the same length. Sew together and press the seam.

2 | Pin a new C to the right side of a new B, right sides together, and stitch *(fig. 2)*. Press the seam.

3 | Pin a new C to one A, right sides together, positioning the C along the top left-hand side of A *(fig. 3)*. Sew together and press the seam.

4 | Pin a second C to the bottom left-hand side of the same A, right sides together *(fig. 4)*. Sew and press the seam.

◀ *fig. 1*

◀ *fig. 2*

◀ *fig. 3*

◀ *fig. 4*

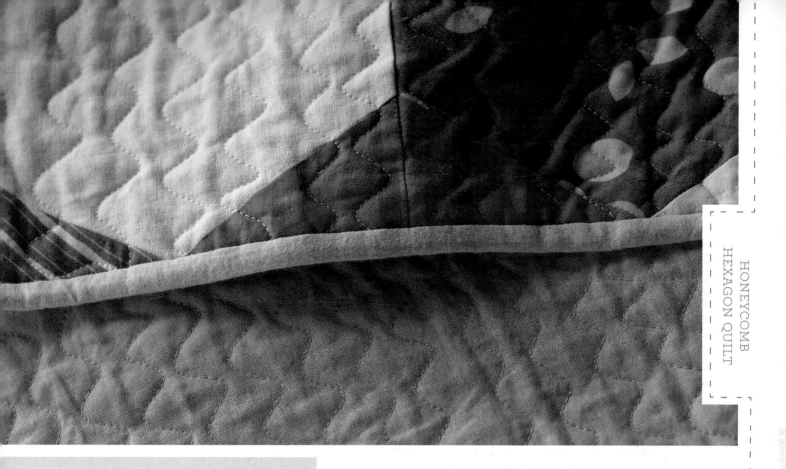

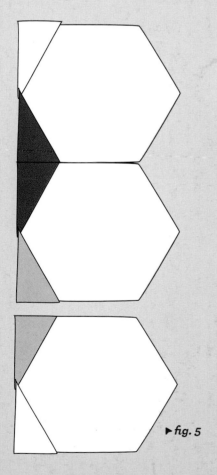

▶ *fig. 5*

*Note: The C triangles attached in Steps 3 and 4 should be different fabrics, but to create the illusion of a row of partial hexagons along the quilt edge, use the same fabric for the bottom left-hand triangle of one hexagon and the top left-hand triangle of the hexagon below it (**fig. 5**).*

5 | Repeat Steps 3 and 4 to make a total of 12 hexagons with C triangle add-ons on the left-hand side.

6 | Repeat Step 3, this time pinning and stitching the C triangle to the top right-hand edge of the hexagon.

7 | Repeat Step 4, pinning and stitching a new C to the bottom right-hand side of the same hexagon.

8 | Repeat Steps 6 and 7 to make a total of 12 hexagons with triangle add-ons on the right-hand side.

9 | Pin the assembled unit from Step 1 to a unit from Step 5, right sides together.

10 | Beginning at the edge with the triangles, sew the two units together, stopping ¼" (6 mm) short of the hexagon corner, at the seamline intersection (*Fig. 6*). Backstitch and cut the thread. Press the seam.

▲ *Triangles and half-hexagons complete the edges of the quilt.*

11 | Pin another Step 5 unit to the Step 10 unit, right sides together. Sew from the triangle edge to the seamline intersection, as in Step 10. Backstitch and cut the thread; press the seam.

12 | Continue adding Step 5 units, one at a time, to create a strip of 12 hexagons with a half-hexagon at the top and a straight left edge all the way down.

13 | Repeat Steps 9 through 12 for half- and full hexagons with the C triangle add-ons along the right-hand edge, remembering to begin sewing at the triangle edge, stopping ¼" (6 mm) from the hexagon corner, and backstitching to secure the seam.

Making the Interior Rows

Each interior row consists of 12 hexagon patches and 1 half-hexagon patch.

14 | To begin, pin a B to an A, right sides together, along one edge.

15 | Beginning ¼" (6 mm) from the corner by backstitching, sew to the point ¼" (6 mm) from the next corner where the seamlines intersect. Backstitch, cut the thread, and press the seam.

16 | Pin another hexagon (A) to the Step 15 unit. Sew between the seamline intersections, as before, and press the seam.

17 | Continue adding hexagons, one at a time, to make one interior row of 12 hexagons and 1 half-hexagon.

18 | Repeat Steps 14 through 17 to make a total of eleven interior rows.

Putting the Rows Together

19 | To ease sewing rows together, match and pin one pair of edges at a time. Starting with the end row constructed with left-hand triangle add-ons, pin the first edge of that row to the first edge of an interior row, right sides together. Rotate the interior row so it begins with a full hexagon at the top and ends with a half-hexagon at the bottom **(Fig. 7)**.

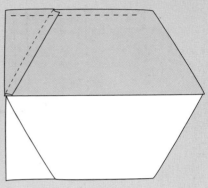

▲ *fig. 6*

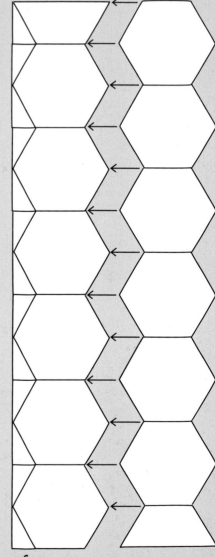

▲ *fig. 7*

Honeycomb Hexagon Quilt

20 | Sew the first edge, beginning at the quilt's top edge and stopping ¼" (6 mm) from the next corner, at the seamline intersection. Backstitch to secure the seam; cut the thread. Wait to press the seam after all the edges between the first two rows have been sewn.

21 | Reposition the rows to align the next pair of edges. Starting ¼" (6 mm) from the first corner of the second edge (the seamline intersection) with backstitches, sew all the way to the next seamline intersection. Backstitch to secure the seam and cut the thread.

22 | Continue pinning and the sewing edges along the row. End the final seam not at the seamline intersection, but at the quilt's bottom raw edge. Press the seams.

23 | Pin and sew the third row to the first two, right sides together, remembering to pin and sew one edge at a time. Notice that the third row begins with a half-hexagon at the top and ends with a full hexagon at the bottom. Begin and end each seam at the seamline intersections; the exceptions are the first and last seams, which continue to the quilt raw edges. Backstitch at the beginning and end of each seam. When the row is complete, press the seams.

▲ *Left: Rows of hexagons in prints and solids; right: detail of quilt backing and binding.*

24 | Continue adding rows, one row at a time, alternating half- and whole hexagons at the top, until all the rows are sewn together and the top is complete. The final row added is the other end row, where triangles were sewn to the right-hand edges of the patches.

Finishing the Quilt

See pages 17–33 for detailed instructions on basting, quilting, trimming, binding, and labeling the quilt if desired.

25 | Pin the 2 pieces of backing fabric, right sides together, along one long edge. Sew together and press the seam open, to yield a 90" (229 cm) square backing.

26 | Lay the backing fabric, wrong side up, on a flat work surface. Smooth the fabric outward from the center and secure it by taping the backing edges to the work surface with masking tape. The backing should be taut but not stretched.

27 | Lay the batting on the secured backing and smooth to remove wrinkles. Center the pieced top on the batting and backing, smoothing it outward from the center. Pin-baste the quilt layers.

28 | Machine or handquilt as desired. For a large quilt such as this one, you may wish to investigate renting time on a long-arm quilting machine (see sidebar, page 149). I quilted my Honeycomb Hexagon with zigzagging rows of stitches about 1" (2.5 cm) wide and 1" (2.5 cm) apart across the entire quilt width.

29 | Trim the backing and batting to match the quilt top.

30 | Using diagonal seams, sew the binding strips together and bind the quilt.

renting time on a *long-arm quilting machine*

→ A small quilt or pillow top is easy and fun to stitch on a home sewing machine. Quilting a bed-size quilt on a sewing machine is not impossible, but maneuvering a large top is difficult and requires a huge time commitment.

My solution to this dilemma is to rent time on a long-arm quilting machine, a large freestanding sewing machine made for professional quilters. This machine has a much larger throat than a standard machine and a room-size span. Two separate rollers hold the quilt taut as you maneuver the stitching apparatus across the surface of the machine. The quilt layers are attached to the rollers, eliminating the need for basting. As you quilt and finish each section, you then roll it toward the back roller with the aid of an electric motor. Because of the speed of the stitching, and no basting, even a novice can densely stitch a large-scale top in four to six hours. And because the quilt is always perfectly held between the rollers, you'll have no puckers in the back of the quilt. It's miraculous!

Long-arm quilting machines are large and expensive, so I rent one by the hour. Many quilt shops and individual long-arm owners offset the cost of the machine through rental. To find one, call local quilt and fabric stores; if they don't rent, ask if they know of someone who does. Or ask a fellow quilter or sewer. If you still come up empty-handed, type "long-arm rentals" and your city into a search engine and let the Internet solve your problem.

Once you've located a willing renter, ask about an introduction class. A long-arm quilting machine is not difficult to master, but there are some things you'll need to know, and it's a good idea to practice before you quilt your masterpiece. Once you're ready to quilt, most long-arm machine owners charge by the hour, but the rental fee might not include thread. Ask about any additional fees.

I've found that the price of renting is very reasonable, and the speed and ease of working on a long-arm machine makes quilting a large top easy, quick, and enjoyable.

◀ *Long-arm machine by Jessica Hartman, from Wikipedia.com*

*templates

**FOUR POINTS TOTE
BAG TEMPLATE**
*enlarge 200%
¼" (6 mm) seam allowance included
see project on page 90*

place on fold

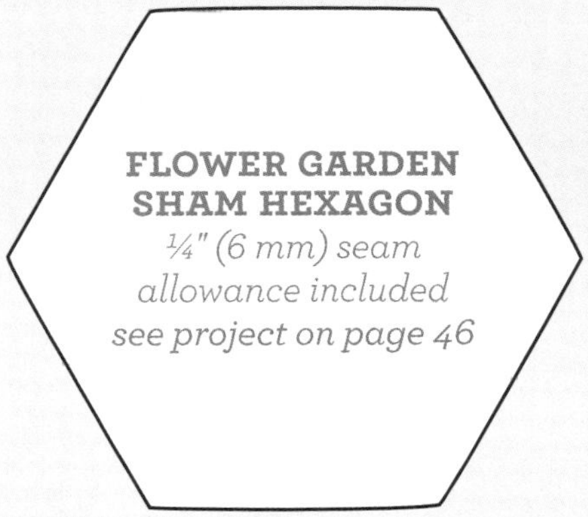

**FLOWER GARDEN
SHAM HEXAGON**
*¼" (6 mm) seam
allowance included
see project on page 46*

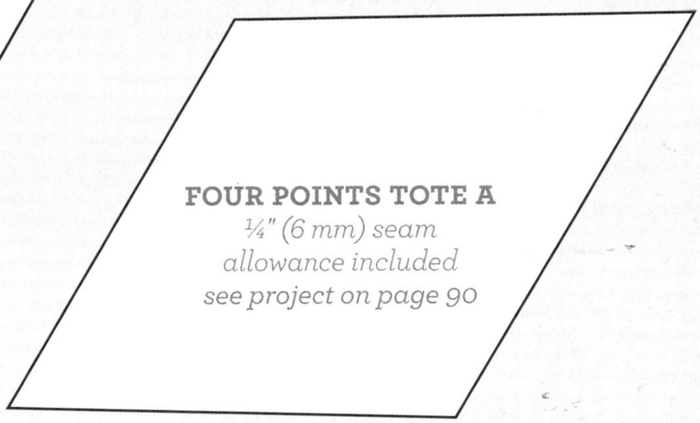

FOUR POINTS TOTE A
*¼" (6 mm) seam
allowance included
see project on page 90*

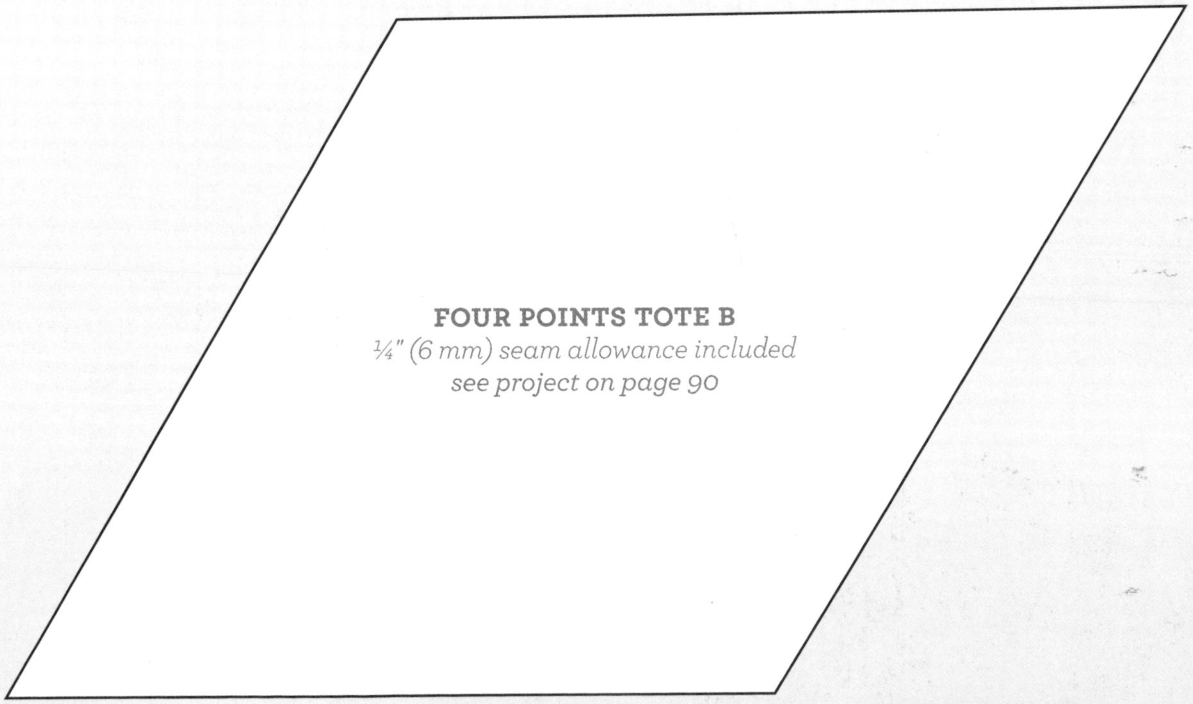

FOUR POINTS TOTE B
*¼" (6 mm) seam allowance included
see project on page 90*

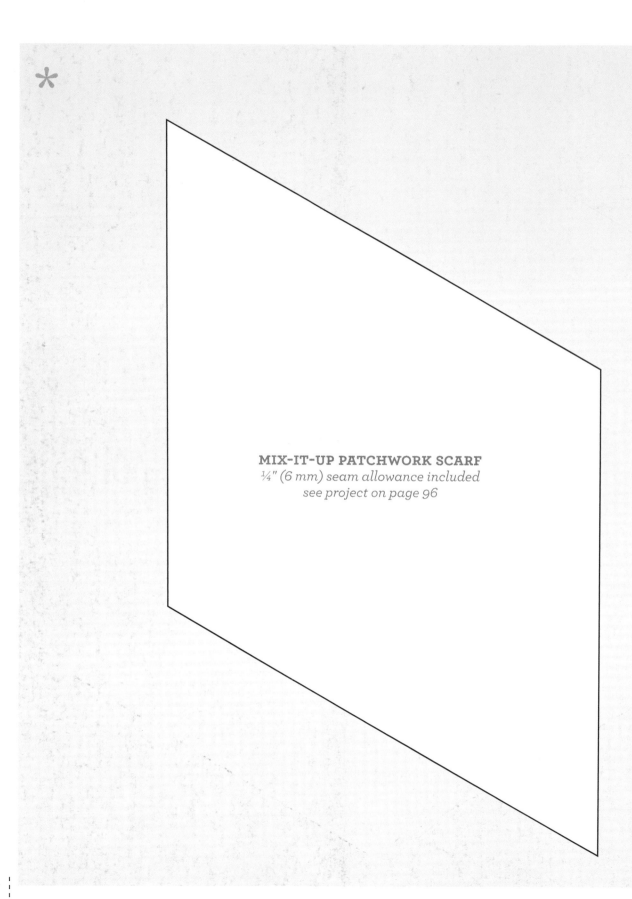

MIX-IT-UP PATCHWORK SCARF
¼" (6 mm) seam allowance included
see project on page 96

HONEYCOMB HEXAGON A
¼" (6 mm) seam allowance included
see project on page 142

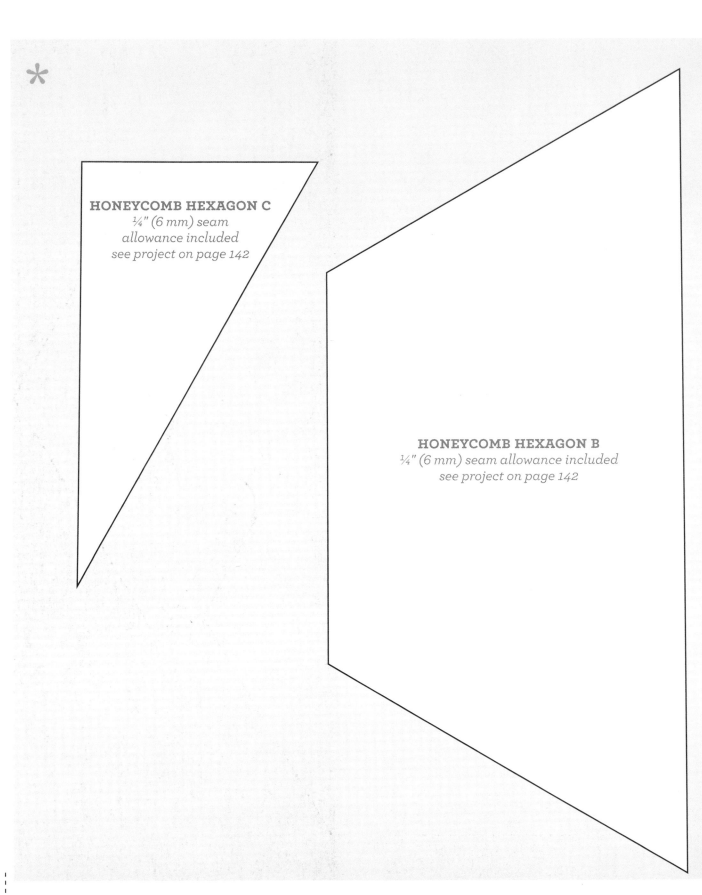

HONEYCOMB HEXAGON C
*¼" (6 mm) seam
allowance included
see project on page 142*

HONEYCOMB HEXAGON B
*¼" (6 mm) seam allowance included
see project on page 142*

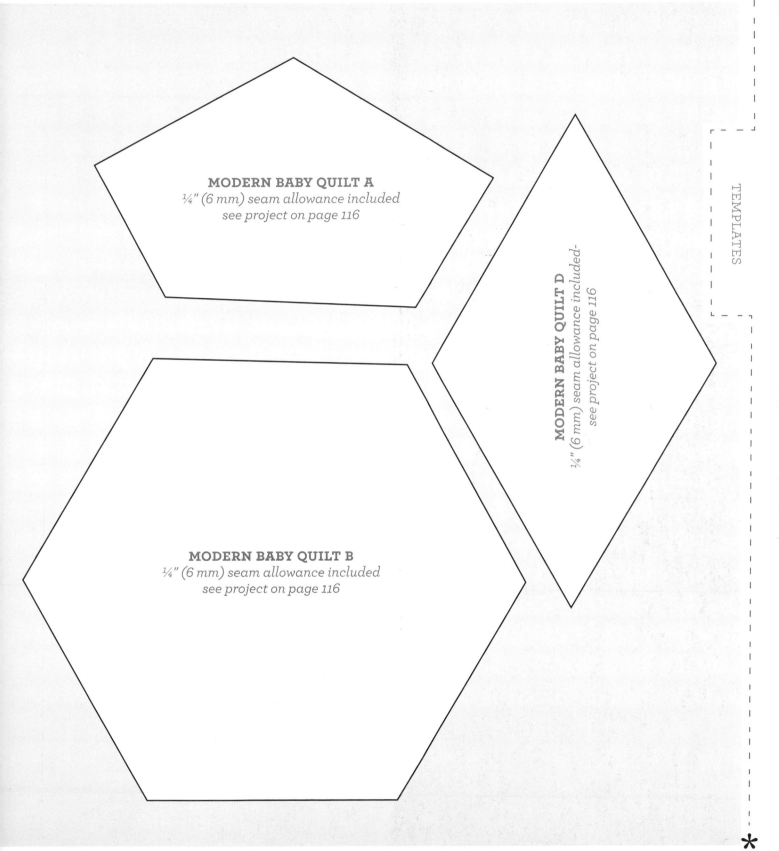

MODERN BABY QUILT A
¼" (6 mm) seam allowance included
see project on page 116

MODERN BABY QUILT D
¼" (6 mm) seam allowance included-
see project on page 116

MODERN BABY QUILT B
¼" (6 mm) seam allowance included
see project on page 116

TEMPLATES

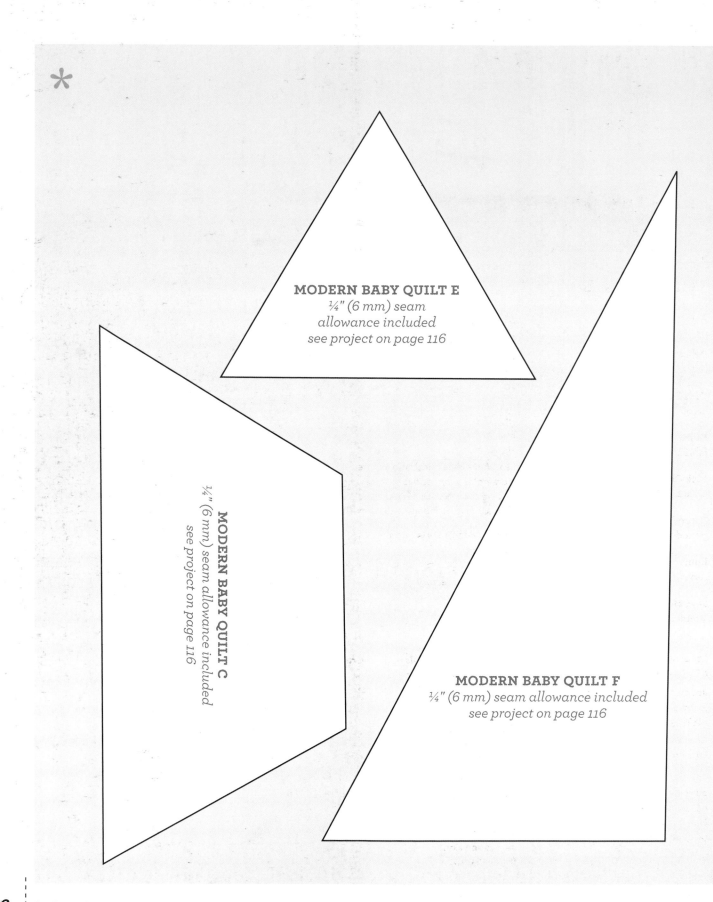

MODERN BABY QUILT E
¼" (6 mm) seam
allowance included
see project on page 116

MODERN BABY QUILT C
¼" (6 mm) seam allowance included
see project on page 116

MODERN BABY QUILT F
¼" (6 mm) seam allowance included
see project on page 116

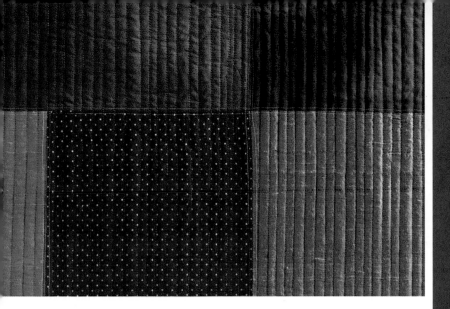

resources

Internet-only Fabric Sources

Bolt 44
bolt44.com

Cia's Palette
ciaspalette.com

Fabric.com
fabric.com

Pink Chalk Fabrics
pinkchalkfabrics.com

Reprodepot Fabrics
reprodepot.com

Runner Girl Fabric
runnergirlfabric.com

Sew, Mama, Sew
sewmamasew.com

Internet + Retail Fabric Sources

Joann's Fabric and Crafts
joann.com
(888) 739-4120
*Check local directory
for store location.*

Purl
purlsoho.com
459 Broome St.
New York, NY 10013
(212) 420-8796

Sources for Japanese Fabrics

Matatabi Japanese Fabric
etsy.com/shop/Matatabi

Sweet Flavor Fabrics + Accessories
etsy.com/shop/sweetflavor

Notions

Etsy
etsy.com
*Search Etsy, the handmade online
marketplace, for notions such as
zippers, vintage and new buttons,
clasps, buckles, ribbons, and trims.*

Joann's Fabric and Crafts
joann.com
(888) 739-4120
*Check local directory
for store location.*

Wooden Handles for Four Points Tote

*The handles used in this project were
found in a thrift store, but the following vendors sell wooden handles in
similar style.*

Addicted to Crafts
addictedtocrafts.com
(253) 925-5200

Create for Less
createforless.com
(866) 333-4463

Yarn Supply
yarnsupply.com
(800) 235-1577

bibliography

Crow, Nancy. *Nancy Crow*. Elmhurst, Illinois: Breckling Press, 2000.

Granick, Eve Wheatcroft. *The Amish Quilt*. Intercourse, Pennsylvania: Good Books, 1989.

Fasset, Kaffe. *Passionate Patchwork*. Newton, Connecticut: The Taunton Press, 2001.

Fisher, Laura. *Quilts of Illusion*. New York: Sterling Publishing, 1990.

Gillow, John and Nicholas Barnard. *Traditional Indian Textiles*. New York: Thames and Hudson, 1991.

James, Michael. *Michael James Art and Inspirations*. Lafayette, California: C&T Publishing, 1998.

Jinzenji, Yoshiko. *Simple Quilt: Yoshiko Jinzenji's White Design*. NHK Publishing, 2005.

Leon, Eli. *Who'd a Thought it: Improvisation in African-American Quiltmaking*. San Francisco, California: San Francisco Craft and Folk Art Museum, 1987.

Meurant, Georges. *Shoowa Design: African Textiles from the Kingdom of Kuba*. New York: Thames and Hudson, 1986.

Schmidt, Denyse. *Denyse Schmidt Quilts: 30 Colorful Quilt and Patchwork Projects*. San Francisco, California: Chronicle Books, 2005.

Wahlman, Maude Southwell. *Signs and Symbols: African Images in African American Quilts*. New York: Studio Books, 1993.

Watts, Katherine. *Anna Williams: Her Quilts and Influences*. Paducah, Kentucky: American Quilter's Society, 1995.

index

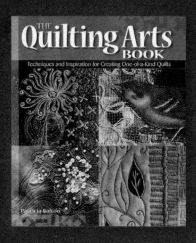